The Authentic Servant

IN MARK'S GOSPEL

VICTOR MAXWELL

AMBASSADOR

Greenville • Belfast

The **Authentic Servant**
© 1996 Victor Maxwell

ISBN 1 898787 58 1

Published by

AMBASSADOR PRODUCTIONS, LTD.
Providence House
16 Hillview Avenue,
Belfast, BT5 6JR

Emerald House
1 Chick Springs Road, Suite 102
Greenville, South Carolina, 29609

LIST OF
Contents

Good News From Mark

S aints are not exempt from suffering nor alien to tears. They may be saved by the grace of God but not necessarily spared from the pain and distress of persecution or the grief and torment of adversity. From the cruel and remote pogroms of Soviet Russia to the blood-stained heather of bonnie Scotland, saints and martyrs have been tortured, stoned, burned and in many other wickedly devised ways paid the ultimate price of love for Christ.

Such suffering of the godly is not new. From the stoning of Stephen, the first Christian martyr in the first century, every generation of Christianity has known those who gained the martyr's crown. Their blood has often been "the seed of the church."

In two thousand years of church history there probably was no community of Christians who suffered more than those of the first century. Christians were disowned, despised and often disenfranchised of their families and properties by religious Jews. They were made the objects of scorn and derision by the philosophical Greeks who conceitedly presumed they were the guardians of all true knowledge. To the secular Romans Christianity was considered to be a sect of Judaism, and their confessed adoration of Jesus Christ as God was taken as rivalry to the deifying of Caesar and a threat to the political might and power of the Roman Empire. To be a Christian in such a tyrannical age of persecution left no room for insincerity or easy-believism. Devotion to Jesus Christ meant sacrifice, suffering, tears and often death. It is not surprising that many of these persecuted saints fainted under the burden and strain of severe persecution and wavered in their faith.

It was to this community of distressed saints in such a tumultuous time that Mark set forth a vivid portrait of Jesus Christ as the Suffering Servant of God. This was Good News from Mark. His Good News was all about Jesus Christ who came not to be served but to serve and to give His life as a ransom for many. He is the Self-giving One and yet the sovereign Lord. The setting of oppression and persecution shaped Mark's writings. As the writer to the Hebrews admonished his readers to "Consider Him lest you be weary and faint in your minds," (Hebrews 12:3) so Mark's portrait of the suffering Saviour was to encourage Christians who felt crushed and overcome by constant oppression.

Mark was not an historian nor a biographer. Mark was a preacher, a theologian who communicated his message by the pen not only to the blessing of his contemporaries but also to succeeding generations. Initially he summarised who Jesus Christ is, and then to support the statement, in sixteen fast moving and action packed chapters, he skilfully pieced together events and sayings in the ministry and life of our Lord in such a way that they confirmed Mark's initial announcement. Jesus Christ is the Son of God and the Good News is authentic because of Who Jesus is.

Although written almost two thousand years ago, this Good News from Mark not only bears the imprint of divine authenticity, it comes with freshness to meet us where we are today. In our "get and grab" age of materialism and the vain world of egotism and self projection, it is both stimulating and challenging to face the paradoxical sayings of our peerless Lord. *The last shall be first, to give is to* receive; *in dying we live; losing is finding; the least shall be the greatest; poverty is riches; weakness is strength and serving is reigning.* Mark takes these paradoxes and dynamically displays them in the life of our Lord and His followers. The heart of the Saviour's mission was His death on the cross and beyond the cross — the resurrection.

Here is good news for modern man. The Gospel is true. Jesus Christ is the Son of God. Sin and death have been defeated by Christ's sacrifice on the cross. He rose triumphantly, and soon He is coming again. Keep on believing in Him in spite of the persecution. Keep on loving Him whatever men may say. Keep on serving Him whatever the cost. Keep on preaching Christ, for He will triumph, and we will conquer with Him.

I am grateful to the continued patience of my wife Audrey who often was left alone while I gave attention to this book. She has been a true and loving help meet in all our service for Christ. My thanks also to Tomm Knutson, my son-in-law, for again taking time and effort to edit the original manuscript and to Heather Knutson and Vivian Knutson for doing the proof reading. Our daughters Sharon and Heather have been a constant source of inspiration and encouragement. I am also grateful to all the friends at Templemore Hall with whom we shared in the ministry of God's Word as we studied the Gospel according to Mark. To family and friends I say, "Keep on believing in Jesus Christ; keep on loving the Saviour; keep on following the Master, and keep on serving our matchless Lord."

CHAPTER ONE

The Gospel According To Mark

I recently received an invitation to conduct a series of Bible studies with the Apurinã Indians located in the region of the River Purus, one of the great tributaries of Brazil's mighty Amazon River. Only in recent years have these indigenous people had the opportunity to hear the Gospel of the Lord Jesus, and even more recently have they received the first translation of part of the Scriptures in their own tongue. Judy King and Cathie Aberdour have spent years living with these Indians in their natural habitat, learning their language, reducing it to writing, teaching the Apurinã s how to read and write and then labouriously translating the Scriptures into their language. You can appreciate this is not the work of short term missionary endeavour. Rather, it has been a life work of dedicated service. As promised, the good seed of God's Word has produced a harvest. Planted here and there near to the River Purus are small congregations of Apurinã Christians.

Judy and Cathie began their translating work with the Gospel according to Mark. In view of the invitation I have received to conduct Bible studies, I have tried to imagine what it must be like for a person reading the Gospel for the first time and then having only one book of the Bible. I soon realised that without knowing it, these indigenous people of the Amazon have something in common with many Romans who lived in the first century. The first written record early Christians had of the life and ministry of Jesus Christ was from the pen of Mark, for his was the first of the four Gospels to be written. Of course, the big difference between the Apurinã s and the Romans is that the latter had available the Old Testament Scriptures as a backdrop to the New Testament message.

I mention the Romans because it is generally understood that Mark not only wrote this first Gospel in Rome but also addressed it to the Romans who were increasingly influenced by the missionary endeavours of the early Church. The Romans, ever men of action and strength, had dominated and conquered the world. Through their global power they had introduced their laws, and without mercy they had enforced their justice. Caesar declared himself to be god and demanded allegiance and obedience from the subjugated people. Those who refused to bow to Caesar were often burned as human torches or thrown to lions in the Roman Coliseums.

Courageously Mark took his pen in hand to send forth good news to those who had been subject to Caesar's cruel sceptre. This good news was about One who is greater than Caesar, One whose Kingdom is larger than that of Rome and One who, rather than reign as a dictator and oppressor of people, is characterised by His service and sacrifice for the subjects of His Kingdom. The benefits of His rule brought grace, mercy, peace and the assurance of everlasting life to all who believed on Him, Jesus Christ. The people were weary of dictators and oppression. Mark pointedly set forth Jesus Christ as the Servant, not the servant of men, but rather the Servant of God and the Saviour of men.

Early church fathers inform us that Mark actually gave Peter's account of the Gospel. Some tell us that he got the facts of the Gospel from Peter's preaching, but his insights and explanation of the Gospel came from Paul. Mark was not an apostle (one who was personally called and taught by Jesus Christ) himself but was closely involved with both of these great apostles of Jesus Christ.

Bearing in mind the people to whom Mark was writing and the source of his information, it is not surprising that Mark's Gospel is brief and blunt. He is not given to verbosity. His is the shortest of of the four Gospel accounts, and yet he tells of more events and miracles in the life of Chirst than the other Gospel writers. His writing is concise and compact, pertinent and pithy, effectively conveying the energy and activity of our Saviour's service and sacrifice. Mark's choice of words and change of events makes the two hour reading of the sixteen chapters fast-moving and thrilling. His use of the words "immediately" and "straightway" which occur on forty-two occasions, add urgency to the action. Dr. Vernon McGee draws attention to the fact that Mark uses the little conjunction "and" to such an extent that if it were used with the same frequency in a modern English college test, the student would flunk the exam! However, Mark uses the little connecting word 1331 times in sixteen chapters with such potency that it actually adds colour to the action and urgency of the Saviour's service.

None of the Gospels are complete biographies of the life of our Lord. Each one is a different account of His life and ministry written from different aspects and with different emphasis because they were written by different people.

Matthew, the former Tax Collector, wrote primarily but not exclusively to Jews. He emphasised Jesus Christ as the Messiah and King of the Jews. To affirm the credentials of the Saviour's Kingship and Messianic role, Matthew began his Gospel account with a genealogy.

Luke, "the beloved physician," like Mark was not an Apostle. He had travelled extensively with Paul and wrote with the people of the nations in mind. He began his account of the life of Christ with a case history of the Saviour's birth and went on to highlight the flawlessness of Jesus Christ as the Perfect Man.

John, the beloved disciple and fisherman from Galilee, wrote at a time when the Church was assailed by heresy from Greek philosophers who would have robbed Jesus Christ of His essential deity. With this in mind he reached back to begin with eternity and presented Christ as the Everlasting Word, the Creator of all things with God and equal to God for He is God. John, having initially affirmed his position, proceeded to confirm the statement by setting forth the sayings and signs of Jesus Christ the Son of God.

Mark, the young friend of Simon Peter, addressed the energetic and active Romans. He began his account of the Gospel with Christ's activity and put the spotlight on the toil and travail of the Saviour as the Servant Who came to do His Father's will. This emphasis is well expressed in Mark 10:45 and is the key verse which summarises the message of the whole book, "For even the Son of man came not to be ministered unto, but to minister, and to give His life a ransom for many."

There are many mysteries surrounding our glorious Saviour. One of these mysteries is that although He was the Lord of glory, yet he not only became a man, he also became the servant of men. He was girded with the regal robes in the excellency of His Kingship, yet at the dirty feet of His followers He girded Himself with the towel of a humble Servant and washed their dirty feet, even the feet of the man who would soon betray Him.

Richard Collier's book about William Booth, the famed founder of the Salvation Army, "A General Next to God," gives a lovely story which illustrates the humble example of our Lord.

"In 1878 when William Booth's Salvation Army had just been so named, men from all over the world began to enlist. One man who had once dreamed of himself as a bishop, crossed the Atlantic from America to England to enlist. He was a Methodist minister, Samuel Logan Brengle. And now he turned from a fine pastorate to join Booth's Salvation Army. Brengle later became the Army's first American-born commissioner, but at first Booth accepted his services reluctantly and grudgingly. Booth said to Brengle, "You've been your own boss too long." And in order to instil humility in

Brengle, he set him to work cleaning the boots of the other trainees. Brengle said to himself, "Have I followed my fancy across the Atlantic in order to black boots?" Then, as in a vision, he saw Jesus bending over the feet of rough, unlettered fishermen. "Lord," he whispered, "You washed their feet; I will black their boots."

Mark learned well from the example of the Saviour. He became a servant of Christ. Servants did not speak much of themselves; they spoke of the one whom they served. That is what Mark did. Courageously he took the initiative to do something that no one else had done at that time: provide a written record of the good news of the Saviour. From the Romans of the first century to the Apurinã Indians, who are only now receiving the Gospel, millions have been blessed because Mark wanted to be like Jesus, a faithful servant.

CHAPTER TWO

Mark According To The Gospel

I remember standing in a courtyard of a home in the Armenian part of the walled city of Jerusalem. The home was reputed to be the site of the house of Mary, the mother of John Mark. As we lingered I tried to let my mind fill with the events that took place there. Was it here our Saviour, before He went to the Cross, ate the Last Supper with His disciples? Was it not also here that faithless and frightened disciples gathered behind locked doors on the Sunday after the Saviour's death and were favoured by a visit from the risen Christ? This was the time He spoke of His programme for sending them as the Father had sent Him. And, it was probably in this home that the Apostles, with others, knelt in prayer to wait for the coming of the promised Comforter. What scenes of joy and praise were witnessed in that room when the Holy Spirit came in like "a rushing mighty wind," and all who were gathered were filled by Him. The passion, programme and power of our Lord were probably all exhibited in this upper chamber of Mark's residence.

If all these events took place on the upper floor of Mark's mother's house, then, most certainly, this influence must have greatly impacted and moulded the life of young John Mark. Some commentators think that Mark referred to himself in an anonymous way in Mark 14:51-52. If this were so, then Mark, filled with the zeal and enthusiasm of youth, followed Jesus when all others forsook Him. However, when other young men caught the enthusiastic youth, he left them grasping his linen wrap while he fled naked. What an embarrassing experience for Mark.

Mark's name reflected a blend of the cultures in which he lived. "John" was his Jewish name which is derived from the Hebrew name "Jacob." However, he lived in a Roman society, and "Mark" was his Latin surname by which his influential family was known.(Acts 12:12) His mother may well have been a widow, but the repeated hospitality she gave to the early Church is evidence that Mark came from quite a wealthy family. This was further confirmed when his rich Uncle Barnabas, his mother's brother from Cyprus, sold some land and brought the money to the Apostles for the use of needy saints.

It was because of the influence of this generous uncle that Mark joined Paul and Barnabas after their visit to Jerusalem and accompanied them on Paul's first missionary journey. He must have had some talent to have been permitted by the sending Church to participate in this pioneering missionary endeavour. Pioneer evangelism calls for sacrificial living and self denial. Sadly, Mark could not stick the pace and rigour of the work, at least not at this stage. He was not alone in opting out of his first missionary term. It is a fact of life that a very high percentage of missionaries who go to foreign fields do not survive abroad for more than one term, and many return within the first year. There are many contributing factors that bring about such a high casualty rate. Many factors could have contributed to Mark's early departure from the work.

Some of the reasons that prompt the premature return of outgoing missionaries are:

Physical illness. Life in a foreign climate can be difficult. The rigours of at least two sea crossings on choppy waters and a pitching sea perhaps left Mark seasick. Furthermore, it was known that the coastal area of Perga was rife with malaria and other such diseases to which the young man may have been exposed.

Home-sickness. Only those who have suffered this know what it is like. Perhaps it was the thought of his widowed mother at home and the comforts he had left behind in Jerusalem that made Mark homesick.

Incompatibility. Living and working with other people in close proximity often takes its toll, and some people just cannot get along with their colleagues. This happens with even some gifted and able Christian workers. During the journey Paul had taken the leadership initiative from Uncle Barnabas, and maybe Mark found Paul's regime too strict and arduous.

Insecurity. The "life of faith" seems to be too insecure for some workers. Today many mission agencies have had to cut their budget and reduce the allowance to their workers. The result of this has been that some workers have had to leave the agency. In the cool of the night or even while at sea Mark might have been wrestling with his thoughts and found that an uncertain future in this work was too frightening. He had always been used to security.

Prejudice. Missionaries who arrive in a foreign culture and try to impose their own prejudices without having Biblical foundations with which to back them up often don't stay too long. It has even been suggested that Mark could not contemplate taking the Gospel to Gentile cities thus betraying his Jewish prejudice and inflexibility.

We are not told what the reasons were. It could have been any of these and possibly other reasons we are not aware of. We do know from Acts 13:13 that after an eventful visit to his uncle's native island of Cyprus and after crossing the narrow strip of rough sea to Perga, John Mark could face no more and returned home to Jerusalem.

Mark's desertion was obviously a very sensitive issue between Paul and Barnabas. We are not told what advice was given to the young man at the time of departure or what message was sent back to the sending church in Jerusalem or Antioch. Later, when Uncle Barnabas insisted on John Mark being given a second chance, Paul refused point blank to let the young nephew join them. The controversy generated over Mark was so acute that these two great men parted company. Barnabas, ever the encourager, took Mark back to his home in Cyprus.

With such a catalogue of failure behind him many would expect this young man to abandon any more ideas of venturing out to serve God. Undoubtedly Mark was familiar with the Old Testament accounts of the great heroes of the faith. Abraham, Moses and David rank among the greatest in any list, yet all of these made serious blunders early in their lives. Eagerly Mark had tried to be like Barnabas, a real servant of God. Alas, he had made a few blunders in the attempt. Initially he had been disgraced when young men pulled off his linen wrap and left him naked on the busy streets of Jerusalem. On his first excursion abroad on missionary service he deserted the work and the workers to return home. Finally, the mention of his name to Paul as a companion resulted in a bitter quarrel between Barnabas and the great apostle. Mark had every reason to be discouraged. However, like the great heroes of the faith, Mark did not give up. Probably Barnabas, who had encouraged so many people that he earned the name "Encouragement," had given him the wise advice, "Never give up." Many great men are heroes, not because they never failed, but because they never gave up. Eventually Mark was to find the role he would play and play it well. He always worked playing the role of second fiddle to others. Just like his Lord he served the Saviour by serving others.

Mark became a companion to Peter

As we discuss heroes of the faith, stop and ask yourself this question, "If I had made a mess of things several times, and yet I wanted to serve the Lord, which of the apostles would I learn most from?" Peter is the obvious answer. Maybe Barnabas had advised Mark to spend some time with Peter. A very close bond formed between them. When Peter was writing his first letter in Rome he affectionately referred to him as "Marcus my son." (1 Peter 5:13) It was this close relationship to Peter which motivated and enabled Mark to write an intimate portrait of the Saviour. Papias, the second century bishop, said that many begged Mark to write down in order all that Peter told the congregations and his friends about the Lord. Today we are glad he took that challenge and did a great work. What a turn around for a young man who at first had failed in following his Lord.

Mark became a comfort to Paul

Paul had known Mark from early in his own ministry and had not been too patient with the young man. It is both to the credit of Paul and of Mark that when the ageing apostle wrote to the believers in Colosse, he recommended that if Mark was to come to them they were to receive him. It was an amazing turn around for the apostle and for the now seasoned John Mark that the last recorded words of the apostle Paul, written from death row in a Roman prison, referred to Mark in the following way, "Take Mark and bring him with thee; for he is profitable unto me for the ministry." (2 Tim. 4:11) For Mark, failure certainly was not final. It need not be for anybody.

Mark became Christ's communicator to the world

The man who failed so often at first dedicated his life to serve all mankind. The challenging record he left of our Saviour's life and ministry was good news for the world and the role model for his own life. He has passed the good news on to us, and his written record is a challenge for us to be servants like the Saviour.

CHAPTER THREE

Let's Start At The Very Beginning

There is a lot to be said for being brief. Abraham Lincoln was cut down early in life in the midst of his greatest work. He may not have been the best educated president of the United States, but he most certainly was one of the most effective. I am told that in Oxford University there hangs a copy of a letter he penned to the mother of a young soldier who was killed at the front lines in the American Civil War. As he draws the touching one-page letter to a close he writes, "I am sorry I have wearied you with so long a letter. I didn't have time to write a shorter one." Being brief is an art to be cultivated, for brevity is often best. Brevity often is pithy, pointed and penetrating.

Mark most certainly had the skill of brevity when it came to summing things up and putting things together. This is evident not only because his is the shortest of the four gospels, but he was able to sum up in a few effective and expressive words what it took the other writers almost a whole chapter to cover. Mark's expertise with the pen makes his first chapter one of the most action packed chapters of the Bible, probably rivalled only by the first chapter of Genesis. With constantly changing scenes and a rapid succession of events, we are conducted right through the ministry of John the

Baptist, the baptism and temptation of our Lord, the call of the disciples and the first year of the Saviour's public ministry. However, in all this crowded content of the chapter there is a conspicuous absence of any genealogy which both Matthew and Luke provide.

For the Jews it was important to trace the royal roots of the king. Luke displayed the pedigree of Christ as the Perfect Man. However, a servant does not need such a lineage or birth certificate; he needs a reference. A servant's abilities and his accomplishments are more important credentials than who his ancestors are.

Mark presented the credentials of Jehovah's Servant, Jesus Christ, with a statement where each word was brimming with meaning: "The beginning of the Gospel of Jesus Christ, the Son of God." (Mark 1:1) In speaking of "the beginning," we all know that this was neither the beginning of John Mark nor of the Lord Jesus.

The Scriptures remind us, "In the beginning was the Word." (John 1:1) This goes back to the dateless beginning in eternity and before the inception of time. Our finite minds cannot grasp this eternal dimension. For us it is enough to know that as far back and as far forward as the human mind can imagine, Christ the Infinite and Eternal Son of God is there; He always has been there and will always be there forever.

The first ten words of the Bible mark the birth of time, "In the beginning God created the heaven and the earth." (Genesis 1:1) One day God will also call for closing time when we all shall be gathered to the great eternity. However, "the beginning of the Gospel of Jesus Christ, the Son of God" dates the beginning of the earthly ministry of our Saviour. This is the time when He entered those three vital and final years of His incarnation.

In Britain the good news of the birth of an heir to the throne and the birthday of the reigning monarch are marked by the familiar twenty-one gun salute. The echo of canon fire hails the good news from the royal palace. The word "gospel" was a well known word in Roman times, for when a ruler began to reign or a son was born to the emperor's family, the announcement was called gospel—good news. The Gospel of Jesus Christ is the best news out of heaven. It tells that God loves the worst of sinners and that Jesus paid our debt on the cross. Now that is good news.

In presenting the credentials of our Saviour, Mark gives the full title, "Jesus Christ, the Son of God." Together these names speak volumes about the Saviour.

The gospel is all about Jesus. Jesus is the name that gives His identity. He was always known as "Jesus of Nazareth." He was a very historical person. Mark gives us the unfolding drama of His life and work, His words of sympathy and forgiveness, and above all, His suffering and death on the cross and His resurrection from the dead by which He has provided salvation for us.

Mark further indicates that this Jesus is also the Christ. "Christ" is the Greek word for "the anointed one" which is a translation of the Hebrew word "Messiah." This name indicates His authority. Anointing in the Old Testament was a frequent practice. Priests, prophets and kings were anointed at the inauguration of their office. However, Israel had long waited for "the Anointed One - the Messiah" Whom God had promised to send as a Priest like Melchisedec, a Prophet like Moses and a King like David. Mark declares that the long awaited Anointed One, the Messiah, is Jesus Christ.

Mark climaxes the credentials of the Lord Jesus by indicating that Jesus is the Son of God. This clearly indicates His divinity. There is no doubt that to Mark, Jesus Christ, was the Son of God, the Creator of all things, the Sustainer of all things, God manifest in the flesh. Paul later wrote that "in Him dwells all the fullness of the Godhead bodily." (Col. 2:9)

Like a lawyer presenting his plea or a preacher his text, so Mark laid the foundation of his writing by furnishing the affirmation about

Jesus in this opening statement. Is Jesus Christ competent to corroborate this claim?

The Apostle Paul later wrote, "This is a faithful saying and worthy of all acceptation, that Christ Jesus came into the world to save sinners of whom I am chief." (1Tim. 1:15) Paul had no doubts about the credentials of the Saviour. In concise terms he expressed what the Gospel was, "Christ Jesus came into the world to save sinners." That is good news. He then spoke of his experience of the Gospel in his own life, "this is a faithful (proved) saying." He proved it in his life, for the Gospel had changed him from a blaspheming persecutor of the church to make him the foremost preacher of the Gospel. On this basis Paul exhorted others to prove the Good News for it "is worthy of all acceptation." This had given Paul a new beginning. It did the same for Mark and will do the same for you also if you come to Jesus Christ the Son of God.

CHAPTER FOUR

All About Jesus

MARK CHAPTER 1 VERSES 2-13

L ike a seamstress picking up some loose ends that have lain untouched for a long time, Mark reaches back to the closing chapter of the Old Testament and picks up the golden thread of Messianic promise that had been left in abeyance for more than four hundred years. With this thread he interlaces the opening scenes of the life of Christ to produce a rich picture of Jehovah's Servant. The last promise of Malachi's prophecy is that the "Anointed One's" coming will be preceded by the sudden arrival of the prophet Elijah.(Mal.4:5)   To this day Jews in their blindness believe that Elijah will come before Messiah, When they celebrate the Passover they prepare a cup of wine for Elijah and leave a vacant chair just in case he should arrive during the meal.

Giving continuity to the precious strand of Messianic promise and making it serve as a link between the last book written in the Old Testament and the first of the Gospels in the New Testament, Mark, with characteristic suddenness, presents John the Baptist as the fulfilment of that promise. As a needle piercing through cloth making way for the thread, so John came as the forerunner of the Saviour. His ministry was penetrating and pricked the conscience of a sinful generation and yet, as the needle of a compass finds its magnetic field, so John always pointed the lost to Jesus Christ. Mark introduced John the Baptist, then drew other colourful strings together to produce a rich tapestry of our wonderful Saviour in these opening verses.

Jesus Christ was announced by John the Baptist. 1:1-9.

John the Baptizer bursts unto the New Testament page with dynamic freshness. He stood alone and aloof from all other men. Our Saviour said of him that of those born of women there was none greater than John the Baptist. He was the last of the Old Testament prophets and the first of the New Testament evangelists. Away from the ritual of the Temple or the opulence of the Royal Palace, this rugged and rustic servant of God emerged in the wilderness of Judea. It seemed to be the worst of times. The voice of a prophet had not been heard for four hundred years. God was silent. The austerity of John's life seemed to set him against the materialistic and ritualistic spirit of the age. His clothing, his diet, his location and his powerful preaching shook the whole of Judea and beyond. Outside of our Lord Himself, John was probably the greatest preacher that ever lived. When he preached people listened. He had no committee to back him. We read of no colleagues who stood with him and no offerings to finance him. He was a man sent from God and filled with God. Our Sovereign Lord reserved His best servant for the worst of times. He always does.

As a brave pioneer John prepared the way for the coming of the King. With the authority of a fiery prophet he predicted the emergence of the Messiah. With the zeal of an evangelist he pointed sinners to the Lamb of God. With the humility of a servant whose work was accomplished he was content to be eclipsed by His Master.

The authority of John's ministry was the authority of God's Word. It is still the only authority for ministry today. The utility of John's ministry was to be what God wanted him to be. We can aspire to no greater height than to be, and be content, with what God wants us to be. The humility of John's ministry was the abasement of himself and the aggrandisement of the Saviour.

Jesus Christ was anointed by the Holy Spirit.   *1:10*

As John burst forth on the earth with the introduction of the Lord Jesus, God broke through the heavens to identify Him as the Messiah (the Anointed) of God. When Mark referred to "The heavens opened..." he used the same word as was used for "the opening of the veil of the Temple, it was ripped, torn, rent." God tore the heavens open as the Holy Spirit came upon the Lord Jesus with power. In both cases it was God's testimony to the work of His Son. The first breakthrough would be as God came to earth. The second would clear the way for man to go to God. When God ripped open the heavens He testified to the start of the Saviour's ministry. When He rent the veil of the Temple he testified to the success of that ministry.

The Baptism of our Lord is a clear demonstration of the activity of three divine and distinct persons. The Son/Servant standing in the water, the Holy Spirit in the form of a dove descending out of heaven and the Father speaking from heaven. As Trinitarians we do not claim to believe in the triunity of God because we can understand it. We believe it because the Bible teaches it.

This anointing is the fulfilling of Isaiah's prophesy, "The Spirit of the Lord is upon me because He has anointed me to preach..."(Is. 61:1) Everything the Father sent the Son to do He did by the Holy Spirit Who is also known as the Spirit of Christ. Jesus Christ was conceived of the Holy Spirit in the womb of the virgin (Mat.1:20), He was anointed by the Spirit coming out of the waters inaugurating His earthly ministry, (Acts10:38) He was led by the Spirit into the wilderness. (Mark 1:12) He offered Himself through the Spirit as a spotless sacrifice to God. (Heb. 9:14.) Jesus Christ was raised from the dead by the power of the Holy Spirit (Rom.1:4; 8:11) and by the same Spirit he taught His disciples. (Acts 1:2). Today the Saviour still works in us through same Holy Spirit whom He has given us.

Our Saviour called no disciples nor did He do any ministry until after the Holy Spirit anointed Him for the work. How foolish it is for believers who live without the power of the Holy Spirit in their lives.

Jesus Christ was approved by the Father.   1:11

Three times in the ministry of our Lord the Father's voice declares the Father's delight in His Son and each time it was in relation to the Cross. First His voice was heard on the banks of the Jordan as the Servant of Jehovah identified his sin-bearing death in the Baptism of Repentance. This was the Father's testimony to His pleasure in the Saviour. The next time the Father's utterance was heard was atop the Mount of transfiguration where Moses and Elijah had discussed the Saviour's decease. The Father's testimony on the mountain was to the pre-eminence of His Son. (Mat.17:5) Finally, the Father's voice was heard when our Lord, just days before His crucifixion spoke of the death He would die. (John 12:28) This was the Father's testimony to the glory of the Sovereign. (See Psalm 2:6,7.) God's final and powerful declaration of approval of Jesus Christ was the resurrection from the dead when He was declared to be the Son of God with power.

Jesus Christ and His work on the Cross is the delight of the Father's heart and the theme of His constant refrain. How much more should we also make much of our Lord Jesus and His work on the cross.

Jesus Christ was attacked by Satan   1:12,13

At Belfast shipyard great ships are not only made they are taken out to sea for trials. These trials are necessary to prove the worthiness of the vessel. As the Father had testified to His Son so the Holy Spirit drove Christ to the wilderness to be tested by Satan. This was a serious test for the Son of God. It not only proved that He did not sin, it also proved He could not sin for He was God. The time of His temptation was immediately after heaven's approval. The place of the temptation was in the solitary desert where only God would see. The nature of the temptations struck at the deity of our Saviour, the authority of His Word and the glory of His Cross. The result of the temptations of Christ vindicated the worthiness of Jehovah's servant. He was well able to accomplish all the Father asked Him to do.

The temptations of our Lord teach us that temptation in and of itself is not sin. Billy Sunday said, Temptation is the Devil whistling in the keyhole. Sin is when you open the door." The best answer to temptation is that when Satan knocks ask Jesus to open the door. They have met before and Jesus won the battle. We not only have the victory, we have the Victor.

Jesus Christ was aided by angels.   *1:13*

Angels are but God's messengers who minister. Besides aiding Christ in the desert, they also served Him at His birth, at His tomb, at His ascension and will come with Him in glory at Christ's return. These serving spirits keep on helping us.

With a skilful pen Mark has given us a worthy introduction of Jesus Christ as God's Servant. He is well able to accomplish all God's purpose.

CHAPTER FIVE

Then Came Jesus

<u>MARK CHAPTER 1 VERSES 14-45</u>

The late Dr. Oswald J. Smith, pastor of the famous People's Church in Toronto, Canada, was a gifted Bible teacher, an effective evangelist and a man with a clear missionary vision. Besides all these talents Dr. Smith was also a very accomplished hymn writer who composed some of the best loved and enduring Gospel songs of our time. One of my favourites tells the story of blind Bartimaeus who lived in poverty and darkness until the day Jesus came to Jericho. The refrain is based on the words "then Jesus came."

> *When Jesus comes the Tempter's power is broken,*
> *When Jesus comes the tears are wiped away.*
> *He takes the gloom and fills the life with glory,*
> *For all is changed when Jesus comes to stay.*

John the Baptist was seized and imprisoned, thus his short but effective ministry was terminated. With John gone Mark simply states, "Jesus came." What beautiful words! Like the emergence of the sun after the daystar has run its course, so Jesus came. After John the Baptist had fallen to the tyranny of Herod Tetrarch, it was then that Jesus came to Galilee from Judea. What a blessing for the Galileans.

Glancing through the rest of Mark 1, we discover Jesus came as the Master to call His disciples by the shore, as the Holy One to cast out demons from an unclean man in the synagogue, as the Healer who touched multitudes in Peter's home making them whole, as the Intercessor who spent time on the mountain alone with God in spite of His busy ministry, as the sympathising Saviour preaching throughout Galilee and the Friend of all friends who touched and cleansed the despairing man who had been afflicted with leprosy.

Some years ago our family lived near the headquarters of the American Baptist Church which is in Valley Forge, Pennsylvania. The symbol of their denomination is an ox standing between an altar and a yoke. Beneath is the motto, "Ready for service or ready for sacrifice." In this first chapter of Mark the Lord Jesus is ox-like in His activities, busy at work filling the hours doing the Father's will, yet His busyness never robbed the time He spent alone with God. This chapter gives us a picture of a typical Sabbath in the life of our Lord. On the Sabbath morning He went to the synagogue where he read the Scriptures and cast out demons. After the service He was the guest in Peter's home where He ministered to the family. As the sun set multitudes gathered at the door of Peter's house, and Jesus healed them of various diseases. After such a busy day many would have been exhausted, not so with our Lord; early the next morning He left the house and went to the mountainside to be with His Heavenly Father. This glimpse at the life of our Lord should be a rebuke to lazy Christians. At the hour of the service in the synagogue, Jesus was never absent. We could also learn a lesson from the way Jesus often resorted to the solitary place of communion with His Father in the midst of demanding ministry .

Jesus called disciples to follow Him. 1:14-20

The first title the Lord gave His disciples was "fishers of men." This was not the first encounter these disciples had had with the Lord. They had previously been introduced to Him and believed on Him because of the witness of John the Baptist. This was different—a subsequent call to service which underlined the supreme nature of their calling. There is no greater work than winning souls for Christ. (Prov.11:30) When D.L Moody felt the call of God on his life he promised to speak to at least one soul everyday about the Saviour. One day tired out with his service for God, Moody retired to bed and then remembered he had not witnessed that day to one soul. He jumped out of bed, quickly got dressed and hurried out to the street. There he met a man leaning against a lamppost. Moody spoke to the man about the Saviour. "Mind your own business!" snapped the man. "That is my business," replied Mr. Moody. Three months later the same man pounded on Moody's door late at night and asked Moody to lead him to Christ.

The chosing of the disciples was not just a supreme calling, it was also a surprise choice. These were ordinary fishermen. They had not been to the best rabbinical schools of that day nor did they have clout in the religious world. They had been engaged in ordinary work, washing nets, mending nets and at times casting nets. These are the men whom God called. We should not marvel at this for he still calls ordinary men and equips them to do an extraordinary job. The surprise choice that Jesus made was accompanied by the sublime promise, "I will make you." The word translated "make" is actually the word "create." Jesus Christ, the great Creator, promised to remake each of these whom He had called. John 1:42 tells us that Jesus said to Simon, "Thou art Simon... thou shalt be... Peter." Jesus Christ transformed the fickle life and will of Peter to make a him a mighty fisher of men. He transformed the life of John, a "son of thunder," and made him the apostle of love. Think not of how weak you are. Trust in what God can make you to be.

For this supreme calling Jesus Christ laid down one solitary condition, "Follow Me." To follow Christ involves the forsaking of our own will. It demands that we put Christ first in all things, and then we simply follow Him. The conditions today have not changed. We cannot be "fishers of men" without being followers of Christ. It also is true we cannot be followers of Christ without being fishers of men. Make your business to be wise and wins souls for the Saviour.

Jesus cast out demons in the synagogue. 1:21-28

Capernaum was not the most important centre of Judaism, but it was there that Christ centred His Galilean ministry, and it was there He attended the synagogue.

I love to hear great preachers, and often I think what it must have been like to have heard Spurgeon or Whitefield. Imagine being in Capernaum that Sabbath when Jesus stood to read the Law. There must have been rapt attention. He spoke with authority, and the common people heard him gladly. What a contrast from the dry, boring exercise of the hypocritical Pharisees.

Jesus further demonstrated His authority in the synagogue by His action: He cast demons out of an "unclean man." How many services this man must have attended with no one able to help him, then Jesus came, and that man was rejoicing. However it is sad that the authority and action of our blessed Lord was met with an attitude of critical and hypocritical unbelief. These critics of our Lord had heard His word; they had seen His work, but the Word was not mingled with faith. They were so blinded by prejudice, demons recognised more than they did. Casting out the demons was the first of five great miracles Jesus did in Capernaum. Special condemnation was reserved for that town because they refused to believe in spite of the miracles done there.

Jesus cured diverse people of different diseases. 1:29-34

Peter dared to be different from the unbelieving crowd and took the Saviour home. We all not only need the Lord in our homes, but we should also be sure to take something home from the Lord after we meet around His Word. Peter's home was the home in which God worked. First, the blessing was felt by the family, for the mother-in-law was healed. Second, the blessing of His presence was felt by the friends as multitudes were healed at the door. I love the words, "they brought... He healed." The sufficiency of our blessed Lord was evident for all to see.

Jesus communed with His Father on the mountain. 1:35-39

The Saviour not only had a busy day behind Him, but another full day of preaching lay ahead. We would think that given the circumstances our Saviour would take time off. It is not incorrect to say that Jesus *took* time to pray. But it is more legitimate to say He *made* time to pray! His prayers were in the solitary place. Is it not significant that the disciples who had been with Him in the synagogue failed to accompany him to the solitary place? We must learn to avoid their example, and, like our Lord, make time to pray - close the door to be alone with God. It was here in the solitary place that Jesus drew strength for His service. Take time to consider where Jesus prayed: alone, when Jesus prayed: early and often, why Jesus prayed: His humanity, for what Jesus prayed: for Peter and others. Chopin, the great composer, maintained that if he missed his practice for one day, he knew it; if he missed for two days, musicians knew it; if he missed for three days, the public knew it. Many of the difficulties in our homes and the dryness of barren ministries would be changed if only we learned the example of our Saviour.

Jesus cleansed a despairing man from leprosy. 1:40-45

I think of this story often when I visit some of our good friends at the leprosarium outside the city of Manaus, Brazil. Their joy in just knowing the Saviour is something to see. I can imagine what emotions must have been charging through the man in these verses, for he not only met the Saviour but was also cleansed from his leprosy and asked to keep quiet about it. C. T. Studd, a star cricketer for England, a missionary to China, India and Africa and founder of the Worldwide Evangelisation Crusade, had a passion to win the lost for Christ. As he witnessed with obvious enthusiasm to a lady about the Lord Jesus she asked, "Why are you always trying to talk to me about the Lord?" C.T. Studd replied, "Madam, salvation is like small pox. You can't have it without giving it to others." Some days later Mr. Studd received a telegramme from the same lady that simply stated "I have got a good dose of small pox!"

The man smitten by leprosy had been healed, and Jesus commanded him not to tell anyone. It seems he could not keep quiet, for He disobeyed the Lord and blazed the news abroad. We are commanded to blaze the Gospel abroad, and often we are guilty of disobeying our Lord by holding our peace. As a result of the man's testimony Jesus removed to the desert place where the people came to Him from every quarter.

People coming to the desert to seek Jesus is a magnificent statement about our Lord. When I read the Scriptures I find that all sorts of people came to Him. Not only religious people and rich people came, but the ruins of society also found their way to Christ. They came from all sorts of places. Some came from the temple; some came from their businesses; one man came from up a tree, and a thief came while nailed to a tree. They came with all sorts of problems. They had problems with disease and despair; some were possesed of demons, and others were afraid of death. All who came found that Jesus Christ alone was the answer to their every need. All who came to Jesus found He turned their sunsets into sunrises.

CHAPTER SIX

The Son Of Man Hath Power

MARK CHAPTER 2 VERSES 1-28

T he Gospels are a record of the words and works of our Sav iour. However, what is most important about our Lord Jesus Christ is not the words He spoke or the works He did. These are important. but not the most important. The most important thing about our Saviour is Who He is. He is God. Unless we have a right view of Who He is, then what He did and what He said will lose their value. If Jesus Christ is not Whom He claimed to be, then all He did and all He said was in vain. With unclouded simplicity Mark amply displays Who Jesus Christ is. Our Saviour perceived the need of a paralytic; He saw the faith of his four helpers; He read the thoughts of His critics and was attacked because He exercised His divine right to forgive sins. He called Matthew to the Kingdom and declared Himself to be Lord of the Sabbath. Who but God could do these things? Jesus Christ is God.

Raising the Roof. 2:1-12

Mark uses the conjunction "and" to introduce this chapter and thus give continuity from the previous events. The Saviour had with-drawn from Capernaum into the desert places because of the public-ity spread by the cleansed leprosy victim. When Jesus returned Mark said, "He was in the house." The Portuguese Bible conveys the thought, "He was at home in the house." Obviously this was the house he had left in the previous chapter, Simon Peter's house. The news of His presence had spread quickly, and the house had soon been crowded to the door. But the crowded home had not stopped the sick man. His friends had taken him onto the roof, removed a few tiles and let the man down in a stretcher to the feet of Jesus. In that home Jesus had engaged in His primary ministry: preaching and teaching the Word of God. The principal ministry of the Lord was not to heal and work miracles; these helped authenticate His approval by God as the Servant Prophet.

Grace and authority characterised the ministry of our Lord, and Luke reminds us that the power of the Lord was in Simon Peter's house. This power was manifested in two great miracles. The first was the miracle of raising a paralytic man. A generation ago The Coalmen's Mission in Belfast was a favourite place for Saturday evening gospel rallies. "Wee Sammy" (Dodger) Spence was one of the effective leaders of those Christian Coalmen. He often spoke of the miracle of the man sick of the palsy and how he was healed. Sammy summed up the miracle in typical style, "Here is a man who when he came to the Lord Jesus, he had his head on the bed, but when he left, he had the bed on his head. Now that was a miracle that raised the roof!" The second miracle was even greater. The deepest need of the human heart and the greatest gift that we can receive are summed up in that sweetest of words—forgiveness. Forgiveness for the sinner is a miracle of grace.

Reflect on the weakness of the sick man. Five times we are told he was a paralytic. His condition was helpless and hopeless, and while others could go to Jesus, he had no physical strength to do so. Our Lord, later likened to the Great Physician, diagnosed his greater problem. The man was a sinner.

Consider the willingness of his friends. Four friends, possibly neighbours, were moved when they saw the paralytic's need, and they volunteered to take him to Jesus. Someone suggested we call them, Frank Faith, Larry Love, Harry Hope and Gary Grit. These men epitomised all these attributes. They were not only prepared to take the man to Jesus but to use innovative means to do so. When there was no way in through the door and no entrance through the window, they broke the roof of the house to get the man to Christ. Having got him there, they believed that Jesus was able to heal and forgive him. The Saviour saw their work and honoured their faith. Some traditionalists are so against innovation they seem to be content for people to go to hell.

Ponder the word of the Saviour. "Son, thy sins be forgiven thee." Jesus struck at the root of the man's disease—his sin, and forgave him fully and freely. To the Jewish scribes this statement was a blasphemy and was punishable by death. They had listened with embittered and hostile ears. The danger of criticism and cynicism is that it tells more about the critic than about the person criticised. To the paralytic Jesus' statement was a blessing and changed his whole future. Jesus not only saved the man's life, but also forgave his sin. Besides, the men who raised the roof soon praised the Lord. I am sure the family who owned the house was recompensed for the damaged roof! The Son of God was present; the Word of God was preached; the power of God was evident; the grace of God was abundant, and the glory of God was sounded.

Publicans, sinners and the Great Physician. 2:13-22

The call of Matthew was simple yet sublime—"Jesus saw Matthew." He saw all of Matthew's past. He saw that Matthew was a publican. Publicans were hated for two reasons: they often fleeced the people, and they represented the Roman authority. Jesus saw all of Matthew's problems yet saw the great potential of this one life. Jesus simply said, "Follow Me," and these two words changed Matthew's life. His was a life of faith, a life of following the Saviour and a fruitful life in which he blessed the world as a writer of the Gospel. What a challenge to reach the lost as he opened his home and brought in publicans and sinners; none of the noble men of the town were there. It is interesting that the words "publicans and sinners" are used three times, and each time, publicans come first.

There was not a religious man among them. To this Jesus said, "They that are whole have no need of the physician but they that are sick." (Mark 2:17)

In the Old Testament Jeremiah posed the question, "Is there no balm in Gilead; is there no physician there?" (Jeremiah 8:22) Jesus Christ gave the answer in the New Testament. He said He was come as the Physician of our sin-sick souls. When we go to the doctor, there are four qualifications he must pass in the mind of the patient. Let's apply them to our Physician Saviour.

Is this Physician aware of our problem? Someone once said: if you want to know the best about a man, speak to his pastor; if you want to know the worst about a man, speak to his lawyer; if you want to know the truth about a man, speak to his doctor. Jesus Christ knows the truth about us. He knows our case history and diagnoses our hearts as deceitful, our eyes as blind, our ears as deaf and our feet as going astray.

Is this Physician able to solve our problem? Ask those whom this Physician has touched. Mary Magdalene would tell how He bound up and cleansed her sinful heart, opened her blinded eyes and put a new song on what had been a poisonous tongue.

Is this Physician affordable? Jesus Christ offers salvation and forgiveness freely without charge. In the Gospel we have our healing at the expense of the Great Physician. "Jesus paid it all, all to Him I owe."

Is this Physician available? The Great Physician is only a prayer away. The Bible tells us the Lord is near to all who call upon Him. Whosoever shall call upon the name of the Lord shall be saved.

Do you ever have trouble reading your doctor's prescription? The Great Physician's prescription is easy to read. Do you find medicine hard to take? Repentance may be a bitter pill to swallow, but it leads to the forgiveness which brings great relief.

The Saviour and the Sabbath. 2:23-3:6

The end of chapter two and the beginning of chapter three give two Sabbath day events in the life of our Lord. The first was a secular matter which concerned the disciples plucking corn in the fields. The second was a sacred matter when Jesus healed a man with a withered hand in the synagogue on the Sabbath. In both events Jesus Christ displayed His deity but also engaged the fury of the religious zealots and legalists who held the people in fear and bondage by their traditions.

In the Jewish Mishnah there were 1521 laws relating to the Sabbath. These laws were both extensive and excessive. For example, Jews were forbidden to eat eggs that were laid on the Sabbath. If a man were bitten by an insect on the Sabbath, scratching was prohibited. No false teeth could be used on the Sabbath, and shoes with nails were not to be worn on the Sabbath day.

The Pharisees frequently clashed with our Lord on two matters: the first being that Jesus Christ claimed to be God, and the second concerning His actions on the Sabbath. On the Sabbath our Lord healed many sick; His disciples plucked corn on the Sabbath. This violated the traditions of the Pharisees. Our Lord gave the hypocritical Pharisees a lesson on the use of the Sabbath. Concerning work on the Sabbath, He gave them a lesson on liberty. As regards the word of the law, He gave them a lesson on His Lordship. By doing good to a poor lady in the synagogue, He gave them a lesson on love.

What does the Lord's Day mean to you? Is it a day to enjoy His presence, a day to engage in worship, a day to express our praise, a day to explore His Word, a day to edify our bodies? Alas, today the spirit of the world has invaded the Lord's Day and robbed us of honouring God in the way He instructed us. We should begin the week by meeting with the saints and remembering the Lord Jesus and the miracle of His resurrection. Even Christians have allowed the world and its values to erode their spirituality to such an extent that attendance at the Lord's House on the Lord's Day is often optional. We use our rest day best when we use it for the Lord.

CHAPTER SEVEN

Tough But Tender

There are many amazing features to Brazil's enormous Amazon River. Just a few miles from where we live, the great river converges with its biggest tributary, the Rio Negro. As its name suggests, the waters of the Negro are black, and the waters of the Amazon are muddy brown; where these two great rivers meet, the currents flow side by side for over forty miles in a spectacular and stark contrast of colour. Together they form the one main artery of the River Amazon.

In reading Mark chapter three, I see the flow of the great attributes of our Lord. In Him are displayed the prerogatives of divinity as he heals the sick and gives power to His followers. Truly, He is the Son of God. Yet, flowing alongside His deity is His manifest humanity as He is pressed by the crowd and called by His family. Equally, He is the Son of Man and Son of God. From Him emanated compassion, mercy and grace to the needy, yet He also issued anger and condemnation upon those who trafficked in hypocrisy and empty religion. These attributes are concurrent and complimentary to each other as are all the attributes of God.

This chapter is also a turning point in the ministry of our Lord. Religious Pharisees and political Herodians formed a convenient coalition to plot the destruction of the Lord Jesus. At the same time the popularity of the Saviour extended beyond Galilee, and He appointed twelve apostles whom He prepared for the work of the Gospel.

Observing Pharisees in the synagogue. 3:1-6

Jesus healing the man with the withered hand probably not only took place on the same Sabbath as at the end of the previous chapter, but there is a hint that the legalistic and devious Pharisees actually planted a man with a withered hand in the hope of bringing accusation against our Lord. The atmosphere was tense as Jesus entered the synagogue, and knowing the hearts of all men, He censured the hypocrisy of the wicked hearts and cured the man with the withered hand.

The man with the withered hand. This man must have gone to the synagogue many times and remained virtually unnoticed and little helped by the religionists. They probably had tried to analyse the reason for his handicap but had no power or concern to help him. Only when it served their evil intentions did they make the man a ploy in their sinister plot. Sinners find no succour in empty religion.

The legalists with wicked hearts. Mark tells us "they watched Him," but there is an even more piercing comment which Mark wrote, "And Jesus looked round about on them with anger." Mark records seven looks of our Lord in his narrative, the look of anger (3:5); the look of appraisal (3:34); the look of awareness (5:32); the look of accomplishment (6:41); the look of acknowledgement (7:34); the look of disapproval (8:33); the look of affliction.

Jesus posed a question that highlighted the contrast. He planned good. They plotted evil. He had come with compassion in His heart. They had come with criticism in their hearts. He gave them the truth. They clung to tradition. He came to give life. They sought to take life. Jesus was never angry with publicans or sinners whom the Pharisees despised. What Jesus saw angered Him. He saw the hardness of their unfeeling hearts, the blindness of their bigoted hearts, the hatred in their wicked hearts. It is a sad thing when would-be worshippers come to God's house with hatred, prejudice and hardness in their hearts.

The Lord with His Healing Word. I would rather have been the man with the withered hand who found the Lord to be compassionate and gracious than to have been part of the mob who, with wicked hearts, earned Jesus' condemnation. Much more could be done for the withered hand than for the wicked heart.

Opportunities at the Seaside. 3:7-12

Mark shows that the impact of our Lord's reputation was such that although He withdrew from the Pharisees, He drew the crowds from ever more distant places. Where did they come from? Bible geography helps us understand they came from Galilee in the north, from Judea and Jerusalem in the south, from Idumaea in the east and from Tyre in the west. This amply illustrates the words of our Lord in Matthew 8:11-12, "Many shall come from the east and the west and shall sit down with Abraham and Isaac and Jacob in the Kingdom of heaven, but the children of the Kingdom shall be cast out into outer darkness."

It is also worth noting to Whom the people came. Like a magnetic force drawing all that is caught within its field, Jesus Christ attracted needy people. You can imagine that as the news of His miracles spread, people brought all their sick relatives to meet Jesus and to receive a miracle. So great was the number of those who jostled to touch Him that they pressed in upon the Saviour, and He withdrew again to the safety of a borrowed boat. Here His deity and humanity flowed together. The people did not come so much for the great words Jesus spoke; they were more interested in the great works

He did. He gladly received sinners; He healed the afflicted and liberated those who were possessed by demons.

Having withdrawn from the designs of the Pharisees in the synagogue and from the demands of the people at the seaside, our Saviour withdrew to a mountain to spend time with His Heavenly Father. Busy and demanding ministries must have frequent disengagement for quietness and prayer.

Ordination of His followers on the mountain. 3:13-19

Having engaged in a night of communion and prayer with His Heavenly Father, our Saviour then enlisted twelve ordinary men for a very extraordinary purpose: to be His sent ones. Normally the disciple would choose who his rabbi/teacher would be. Not so with the Saviour. He called each one by name, and He knew them through and through. He was aware of the moods of Peter, the temper of John, the doubts of Thomas and even the deceit of Judas who later betrayed Him. Nearly all of them were from the streets of Galilean towns and were more familiar with fish and boats than occupying a place in rabbinical school. Religious art for centuries has cast the disciples of our Lord into porcelain moulds. But these men were neither porcelain nor plastic saints. All of them were average young men, chosen and changed by the Master. Who were they?

Simon Peter, a married man, was mostly at home with boats and nets, for he was a fisherman. He was foremost among the apostles and was their spokesman. His life ended when he was crucified upside-down in Rome.

Andrew was Peter's brother, and he brought Peter to Christ. He was always bringing others to the Saviour. He was martyred in Greece.

John, like Peter and Andrew, was a fisherman from Bethsaida. He was probably the youngest disciple and was closer to the Lord than any other apostle. He outlived them all and died a natural death although in exile on the Isle of Patmos.

James was John's brother and partner in business. Although he and John were nicknamed "the Sons of Thunder," he, with Peter and John, was one of the inner circle of disciples near to the Lord. James was the first apostle to die, beheaded by Herod.

Philip was a close companion of Andrew. He was a practical man and was always calculating what was needed. He was hanged in Asia.

Bartholomew, also called Nathaniel, always had two opinions about most subjects. He was flayed and beheaded in Armenia.

Thomas, also called Didymus which means twin, was known for his doubts. He became a missionary to India where he was martyred.

Matthew was a tax collector. His literary skills enabled him to chronicle the life of the Lord. He was killed by sword in Ethiopia.

James, the son of Alpheus, was also known as James the Less. He may have been less by name but was of great importance to Jesus. He was sawn asunder in Jerusalem.

Judas Thaddeus distinguished himself from Judas Iscariot. He always pulled his weight and was faithful to his Lord. Sharp arrows made him a martyr in Iraq.

Simon Zelotes had been a political activist. His fiery nature was harnessed and changed by the Lord. He was killed by an angry mob in Persia.

Judas Iscariot was the treasurer and probably the best educated of the group. Our Lord knew him and said he had chosen a devil. He was called son of perdition, and Judas Iscariot is the traitor who betrayed our Lord. He hanged himself.

Our Saviour enlisted them to be with Him. The servant's chief enjoyment is to be with his Master. These men were chosen not only to enjoy His presence but also to be educated by His life. They were with Him at a wedding, with Him in prayer, with Him in the storm, with Him early in His passion, and although they forsook Him, they were with Him after the resurrection and at His ascension. Is it any wonder the Council at Jerusalem took note that these men had been with Jesus? (Acts 4:17)

The Saviour also employed them as messengers to preach. He endued them with power and sent them out. This is not to be confused with the great commission of Mark 15:15-16. On this occasion when Jesus sent them He did not go with them. In the "great commission" He promised never to leave the messenger.

The opposition of His foes. 3:22-30

Professional scribes had been sent from Jerusalem to investigate Jesus of Nazareth who had obviously created a stir in Judaism. As they studied the wonders and miracles He had done and the lives He had changed, they slanderously concluded it was the work of Beelzebub, the Prince of Devils. At this false and villainous accusation our Lord called his accusers and posed a frank question which proved to be unanswerable: "How can Satan cast out Satan?" The Lord Jesus enlarged on the absurdity of their charge and then thrust a two edged word, "Verily I say unto you, all manner of sin shall be forgiven unto the sons of men." Jesus spoke the Gospel when He spoke of unmerited forgiveness of all manner of sin to men. However, the Saviour confronted them with the unpardonable sin, the sin of persistently charging the witness and work of the Holy Spirit and the divinity and Saviourhood of our Lord as the work of Satan. These scribes were in danger of this very sin.

An object lesson with His family. 3:20-35

Mark underlines the pressure of the busy life of our Lord by saying, "And the crowd came together again so that they could not so much as eat bread." His friends thought He was cracking up and sought to take Him from the crowd. His foes schemed to accuse Him. His family came to call Him home. But finally, Jesus emphasised His appraisal of the fellowship that transcends all earthly relationships—the fellowship of God's family.

His physical family. From the periphery His mother and brothers called for Jesus' attention. In response to this call He made a startling statement, "Who is my mother, or my brethren?" Our Lord was not being disrespectful to His family. On the contrary, He addressed His mother from the cross, caring for her welfare, and He appeared to His brothers after His resurrection. The New Testament writers James and Jude were physical brothers of the Saviour. Most certainly there had been a lot of love and affection in that home in Nazareth. It is still important to cherish friendships and care for our family.

His spiritual family. Looking around, Jesus pointed at His disciples and said, "Behold my mother and my brethren!" The Saviour who esteemed His Father's business above earthly food and drink now accounted His spiritual family of greater importance than His physical family. This family relationship has a more permanent bond and a more abiding home. Belonging to the family of God is the highest calling in life. Doing the will of God is the holiest calling in life. Our earthly families are bound with deeper bonds when they are completed by our union with Christ. We do well to sing "I'm so glad I'm a part of the family of God."

CHAPTER EIGHT

Heavenly Stories

MARK CHAPTER 4 VERSES 1-34

In October 1973 Syrian forces secretly converged on the Golan Heights of Northern Galilee. In Israel it was the national holiday of *Yom Kippur*, the Day of Atonement. All commerce was closed. Soldiers were on leave to join their families for this important Jewish Feast. Emergency services throughout Israel were on skeleton staff. With the cunning of a fox and the stealth of a lion, Syria struck at Galilee when Israel was off guard. For twenty four hours Israel reeled as a prey suddenly wakened from sleep. The famous Yom Kippur War is the rest of the story.

The emergence of Jesus Christ in Galilee was even more sensational. Like a shaft of light penetrating the gloom, so was the coming of the Saviour to the sleepy towns of Galilee and the greatest event to ever happen in that area. His miracles had attracted thousands who followed Him wherever He went. The Galilean shore was crammed with those who gathered. Jesus was at the height of His ministry, and it is thought this was the biggest crowd He had addressed until this point. He borrowed a fisherman's boat and used it as an improvised pulpit from which He taught by parables. A story is told of a little boy who was asked to write down his definition of a parable. His written answer was, "A parable is an earthly story with a heavy meaning." He obviously made a spelling mistake, but his definition has some truth. A parable is simply a story put alongside a truth to make the truth better understood. They are what might be called hearing aids. The weight and impact of the stories that Jesus told had a profound effect on His hearers.

Jesus Christ was the greatest story teller of all time. Among His classics are the parables of the Prodigal Son, the Lost Sheep and the Good Samaritan. In His parables our Lord painted word pictures that revealed heaven's truth, but these word pictures were for only those who had "ears to hear." The same parables concealed the truth from those whose hearts were hard with prejudice and whose eyes were closed by ignorance. These pictures that Jesus colourfully sketched were ordinary scenes of life and were like windows through which to see God's truth. They were also levers that pried open the hearts of the hearers to let the light of truth shine in. Of the many parables that Jesus told to the assembled multitude, Mark carefully selected four. The most famous of these is the first, the parable of the sower, the seed and the soil. More verses in the first three Gospels are devoted to this parable than to any other.

The Identity of the Sower.

A farmer sowing in a field was a familiar image for those who lived in the fertile area of Galilee. The Lord called attention to the sower first. Who was this sower? Matthew 13:37 tells us that the Sower is "the Son of Man" and reinforces Mark's portrayal of Jesus as Jehovah's Servant. Jesus constantly disseminated His word in the ears of the masses and also to individuals. He still does. After His resurrection Jesus charged His disciples, "As the Father has sent Me, even so send I you." Jesus commanded us to go into the field with the objective of sowing the good seed of God's Word. Other Scriptures further instruct us that to sow passionately, purposefully and confidently with our eye on the harvest. (Psm. 126:6) We are also to sow plentifully, sometimes broadcasting as in preaching, other times sowing the seed individually as in personal evangelism. (2 Cor. 9:6) Also, like a good farmer, we are to sow with patience, for the seed takes time to mature. (Gal. 6:9)

The Vitality of the Seed

Some years ago while in Egypt I visited the famous Cairo Museum and was astonished with the display of treasure taken from King Tutankhamen's tomb. We learned that along with the gold, silver and precious stones that was buried with the King, archaeologists have also discovered ears of corn that were over three thousand years old. Some of these seeds were planted, and, to the amazement of the archaeologists, the seed sprung up into a small crop. The seed, although hidden for three thousand years, was still living. A seed may appear to be of little value, but it is living and lasting with great potential. So also the Scripture testifies of itself as being living, lasting and powerful just like the tiny seed.

It is appropriate that God's Word was described by Peter as the "incorruptible seed." It is both pure and purifying to sinful men, powerful and empowering to weak men, living and life-giving to dead men. God's Word is the only thing that can take a soul on the way to hell and put it on the road to heaven. God's Word imparts faith to those who hear it. (Rom. 10:17) To those who read and listen, it makes them wise unto salvation. (2 Tim. 3:15) And it is able to save the souls of those who receive it. (James 1:21)

The Word of God was also described by King David as "precious seed." He said it was more precious than gold and sweeter than honey. By this same Word of God the soul is converted, the mind is enlightened, the heart rejoices, and the life is made clean; in obeying God's Word there is great reward. (Psm. 19:7-11)

The Diversity of the Soil.

God's Word is quick, powerful, pure and precious. However, only when the precious Seed is sown will it produce a precious harvest. In the parable there is but one sower and only one type of seed, but the soil is diverse. What was the reason for the diversity? It reflected how people hear God's Word. "And He saith unto them, Take heed what you hear." (Mark 4:24) Jesus Christ placed great importance on how we hear. Thirteen times the word "hear" is used in Mark chapter four. The various soils mentioned in the parable of the sower were probably representative of the hearers in the congregation who listened to the Lord on that day. Hearing the Word of God is the most important thing which can happen to human beings. Jesus wanted the crowd then, and us now, to ask the question, "How do I receive God's Word?"

An intellectual highbrow went to hear the famous American evangelist, D.L. Moody. He took copious notes during Mr. Moody's preaching, and afterwards he said to the evangelist, "Mr. Moody, I noted that you made thirty-eight mistakes in English today." To this the evangelist replied, "I'm sure you are right, but I am using all the knowledge I have for the glory of God. Are you doing the same?" The man had heard Mr. Moody, but he hadn't heard the message.

Some seed fell on the trodden pathway. The hard trampled ground did not allow the seed to penetrate the soil, and the seed was soon stolen away. How easily this happens with the human heart and mind. The Devil uses doubts and distractions as well as many other ploys to steal away God's Word. A trodden-pathway person is not necessarily opposed to God's Word; indifference allows the enemy to steal away God's Word.

Some seed fell on thin soil. It was quickly scorched. Here there is a shallow superficiality in how they receive God's Word. There is remorse without repentance, emotion without conversion, feeling without faith. Alas, too many, too easily receive God's Word in such a fashion.

Some seed fell on thorny soil. In time it was strangled. Too often we allow the weeds of worldly care and doubt to take a deeper root than God's Word, and soon the Seed is crowded out. These weeds soon choke the good Seed.

Some seed fell on trustworthy soil. Here the seed was successful. On prepared soil the seed was productive. We need to prepare our hearts to hear what God is saying. Where the good Seed is sown in good soil, there is always a good harvest. Wherever the Gospel is preached, all these soils are in evidence among those who hear.

Be careful not only what you hear, but also how you hear. The Jewish Shema in Deuteronomy 6:4 is cited in Orthodox Jewish homes at least twice a day and is Judaism's basic confession of faith. The word *Shema* is taken from the first word of the confession, "Hear O Israel." These Orthodox Jews hear the truth, but they do not listen to it. Paul reminded Timothy to "Preach the Word... for the time will come when they will not endure sound doctrine; but after their own lusts shall they heap to themselves teachers having itching ears and they shall turn away their ears from the truth and shall be turned unto fables."(2 Timothy 4:2,3.)

God gave us two eyes to see, two hearing ears that are always open, and one tongue that is housed in a closed mouth and guarded by a set of ivory teeth. Could it be that He wants us to put double emphasis on seeing and listening and much less on speaking?

CHAPTER NINE

The Saviour And The Storm

MARK CHAPTER 4 VERSES 35-41

Two of my missionary colleagues in Acre Gospel Mission, Mark Loney and Sam Scott, were on the Operation Mobilisation ship "Logos 1" when it ran aground on large rocks in the middle of a freezing cold January night in 1988. On that unforgettable night the ship faced strong head winds as they passed through the treacherous Beagle Channel, the graveyard of many vessels, off the southern tip of Latin America. Both young men remember how they were startled from their sleep with the sound of the hull scraping and then a crunch as the ship rammed the rocks. According to Mark and Sam, the dominant memory of that night after all on board the ship were rescued, was the peace and calm that prevailed over everyone in spite of the obvious danger. They proved that no storm nor circumstance which arises is ever greater than our Lord.

Jesus Christ was never lazy or negligent. He always had time for those who needed Him, and this portion of Mark tells us more about how He spent His days. Jesus had had a long day. He had taught the crowds at the shore until the long shadows began to gather and darkness hastened. As the sun set behind the Galilean hills our Lord invited His disciples to pass over to the other side of Lake Gennesaret. He had taught them lessons in parables during the day on dry land;

now He was to teach them by experience in a storm at sea in the middle of the night. They did not know at the time, but the oncoming storm was to prove a most effective lesson about the life of faith.

Often, when visiting Israel, we ask the group where they might like to have been if they had a choice to be present at any time during the ministry of our Lord. We nearly always have the usual variety of answers: Cana of Galilee, Mount of Transfiguration, Upper room, Calvary, Garden Tomb, etc. Never does any one say they would like to have been in the midst of the storm on Galilee. Like the disciples, none of us like storms, yet in the school of Christ, they are part of the course. Without trials and temptations, difficulties and afflictions, failures and tears we would never develop in Christian growth. Spiritual storms are for spiritual enrichment.

> *I asked the Lord that I might grow*
> *In faith and love and every grace,*
> *Might more of His salvation know,*
> *And seek more earnestly His face.*

> *'Twas he who taught me thus to pray*
> *And he I trust has answered prayer*
> *But it has been in such a way*
> *It almost drove me to despair.*

The Master's Presence on the Ship. 4:35-36

Crossing to the other side of the lake was not the disciples' plan. Jesus Christ was the One who gave the invitation. Performing miracles and ministering to multitudes had made it an exhausting day. "He said unto them, 'Let us pass over unto the other side.'" The command to cross to the other side hinted to the fact that Jesus was tired. He withdrew from the multitude. Mark then adds, "They took Him even as He was in the ship." The most important decision taken that night was to make sure Jesus Christ was on board. Mark further adds, "And there were also with Him other little ships." It must have been an impressive sight as this flotilla of small vessels set off to cross the six miles to the other side of Galilee. I think it was the Rev. G. B. Duncan who said, "Jesus Christ was not only the Captain of the boat and the Master of the Sea but also proved to be the Admiral of the fleet, for not one of the craft was lost in spite of the tempestuous seas." Our Lord had not only pointed the direction in which they were to go, but He also guaranteed their safe arrival at the destination.

This is a lovely reflection of salvation and our Saviour's presence with us. The plan of salvation did not originate with us, nor is it performed by us. God is the Author of our salvation, and our salvation was accomplished by the work of Jesus Christ. He gave the invitation, and with Christ on board He guides us in the direction we are to go and guarantees the destination—the Father's House. He never loses His own.

The Menacing Peril of the Storm. 4:37-38

The storm that arose in the night was both sudden and severe. Some commentators think that the storm was a natural phenomenon. Sudden storms were not unusual for the Sea of Galilee. I well remember one day we were to cross from Capernaum to En Geiv on the opposite side; we had not long left the little harbour at Capernaum when gusts of wind suddenly changed what had been a calm sea into choppy waters. The waves started to crash over the bow of the boat. We had to abandon our planned crossing and soon pulled into Tiberias farther down the coast.

The heart-shaped Sea of Galilee is just over six hundred feet below sea level. It is surrounded by high mountains with deep valleys channelled between them. The hot air rising from the sea can create a powerful turbulence on contact with the colder air of the hills. The turbulence of the different pressures produce the winds which are a feature of Galilee.

Other commentators suggest that the storm was a diabolical and Satanic attack on our Lord, and I tend to agree with them. Not only were experienced fishermen sure they would die, but Mark gives a deliberate sense of confrontation between the storm and the Saviour, "And there arose a great storm... and He arose and rebuked the wind." The action of our Lord is amazing. The word suggested is stronger than "rebuke," Jesus "muzzled the wind." Our Adversary may be a roaring lion, but Jesus is well able to muzzle him. He muzzled the lions for Daniel and the storm for His disciples. This was not the first time the Adversary had tried to take the life of our Lord, nor would it be the last.

Although this storm seems to have been diabolical in origin, it certainly was providential for the disciples. They learned lessons they would never forget. They learned that although this storm was sudden to them, it never took the Lord by surprise. When He said, "Let us pass over to the other side," He knew the storm was up ahead. He always knows our storms. He knew this would teach faltering disciples that nothing ever takes God by surprise. Furthermore, the storm was so severe that seasoned fishermen were sure they would die. If these experienced men of the sea feared because they had never seen the like of this, how much greater was the fear of those who were not fishermen? Waves were breaking over the ship's bow, and the boat was filling with water. Add to this scene of danger the darkness of the night. The sense of death seemed imminent and doubts filled their hearts. It certainly was a fearful hour. Nothing sifts out our faith like a storm. The measure of our faith can be gauged in the crisis of a storm. Their faith was measured in the storm, and it registered zero. Jesus knew this would teach them that no storm is ever greater than the Saviour.

There is an irony to this story; although Jesus knew how sudden and severe the storm would be and how the hearts of His disciples would be shot through with fear, He slept. That must have been even more alarming than the storm. Just when they needed Him most, He seemed to be unaware of the emergency, and if He were aware of it, His sleep showed He was indifferent. All of us have times when we think heaven is silent. We often hear, and perhaps we sometimes say, "If God is aware of my distress, why does He not do something?" Driven to the point of despair they did something the wind could not do—they woke the Saviour. They cried in their unbelief, "Carest thou not that we perish?" It is not inconceivable to imagine Peter was the one who voiced these words. He was generally the most vocal of the twelve, and as suggested, Mark drew most of his information from him. The disciples learned that even when it seems heaven is silent, Jesus still cares for us. Peter certainly learned the lesson, for on the night prior to his planned execution in Jerusalem, like his Lord in the crisis on the sea, he slept. Later He wrote, "Casting all you care upon Him, for He careth for you." (1 Peter 5:7)

The Miraculous Power of the Saviour. 4:39

At this darkest and most dangerous hour Jesus arose from His sleep and rebuked the wind and the waves. Mark shows us an eloquent display of humanity and deity combined in the Saviour. He laid His head on a pillow at the rear of the boat and slept such a deep sleep that not even the storm could waken Him. On the same night He stood to command the wind and the sea as the mighty Creator. What a lovely picture of meekness and majesty combined in our Lord Jesus. One minute we see Him being so human; the next minute He is so divine.

Jesus Christ muzzled the wind. When the Saviour was wakened from His sleep, He arose and spoke to the wind. A whisper would have been enough, but in the fury of the angry gale He shouted, not so much that wind could hear Him, but that the fearful disciples might hear His voice. "He rebuked the wind." We miss the sense of authority if we fail to understand the strength of the word "rebuke." It simply means to muzzle. Like a master speaking to a yelping dog, "Stop! Be quiet!" The wind and waves obeyed His command. In the storms of life we also need to hear the word of the Lord.

Jesus Christ mastered the sea. At Galilee Jesus did many miracles. He performed miracles beside the Sea, in the Sea, on the Sea and with the Sea of Galilee. These waters recognised the voice and footprint of their Creator, and immediately as they heard His voice they subsided.

Jesus Christ marvelled at His disciples. "Why is it that you are so fearful? How is it that you have no faith?" This question was sharp and must have pierced the disciples through and through. No one disciple was singled out. They had started the night with faith, but that faith was soon lost overboard in the storm. When faith is jettisoned, then fear reigns. Faith and fear cannot co-exist. Their zero rating on faith was evident because they forgot what Jesus had said. "Let us pass over to the other side." He never said they would go under or turn back. His commands are His enabling. Fear loomed large because they forgot where Jesus was. He was with them in the boat. Children correctly sing "With Christ in the vessel we can smile at the storm." We also should exercise this child-like faith. Terror reigned in their hearts because they misinterpreted what Jesus did. Frequently we are aware that He is in the boat, but we feel He is asleep, or that He is not aware of what is happening. Not so, Jesus slept confidently knowing they were all safe in the Heavenly Father's hand. We also need faith to help us to confidently rest in the storms.

God has not called us to be super heroes who never fail. Here is some good advice. "Learn from the mistakes of others; you will not live long enough to make them all yourself." Some years ago a man wrote a book entitled, **"Great Failures in the Bible."** The book itself was a failure, for nobody bought it. Nobody likes to remember failures; however, failures can be our friends if we learn to employ them properly.

The disciples learned that faith is the antidote to doubt. That night Peter and the other disciples had thrown faith overboard. Doubt brought fear; it always does. Jesus had given them a promise; His presence was with them, and they had seen His power over the elements. Why doubt Him? Peter learned the lesson of faith, for later he wrote, "The trial of your faith, being much more precious than of gold that perisheth, though it be tried by fire." (1Peter 1:7)

The disciples also learned that hasty conclusions are often wrong. They had rashly charged the Saviour with not caring for them. In the light of day they were embarrassed to realise He constantly cared for him. Why worry? Never forget in the day the lessons you have learned in the night.

The Marvellous Peace on the Sea. 4:40-41

"And there was a great calm." In the cool light of the next morning, there was much discussion, and Mark added, "And they were exceedingly fearful and said one to another, What manner of Man is this that even the wind and the sea obey Him?" Does Mark suggest that after the Saviour's rebuke for their lack of faith their fear increased? No. The fear they had in the storm was fear because of the absence of faith. The "exceeding fearful" of which Mark speaks after the storm is that of admiration and reverence at who Jesus Christ is. What manner of Man is this? He is human; therefore, He understands us. Even the wind and the sea obey Him! He is divine; therefore, He undertakes for us.

That night on the Beagle Channel the crew of Christian workers proved that Jesus Christ is still the Master of the sea. "What manner of Man is this?" He is the Creator Saviour and is still the same today. He is with you through your storms.

CHAPTER TEN

What A Wonderful Change In My Life

MARK CHAPTER 5 VERSES 1-43

There appeared in a recent financial journal a full page advertisement in bold print which posed the question, "How much are you worth?" The page also gave space for the reader to tabulate his various assets. Often such a commercial mind-set disregards the fact that the greatest asset we possess is one which cannot be catalogued on paper—an individual life. Until chapter five Mark has portrayed the ministry of our Lord among the multitudes. This chapter teaches us how important individuals are to the Saviour. He purposely pointed the boat in the direction of the Gadarenes and travelled through the fury of a midnight storm just to set one man free who had previously been demented by an army of demons which possessed him. Later, in the midst of a crowd which thronged Him, He took time to heal a desperate woman who had touched the edge of His garment. Finally, at the request of a distraught father, He took time to go to the house of Jairus and call a little girl back from the dead. Each case was one of sheer human tragedy, but on each occasion Jesus saw individuals who were precious to Him.

Dr. Jerry Vines rightly likens this chapter to a visit to "The House of the Incurables." All three cases were beyond human help. In this institution we are first introduced to the male ward and meet a man likely to be classified by men as deranged and beyond psychiatric help. In the female ward the lady would be diagnosed as incurable and terminally ill. All types of medicines had been used on her but without any benefit. Finally, there is a twelve year old girl, but we do not even look for her in the paediatric unit, for she is ready to be embalmed for burial. Humanly speaking all these cases are hopelessly impossible—impossible, that is, without Jesus Christ. Against this back drop of human plight we see the might of the Saviour. With Him there are no impossible situations, He stilled the storm in an hour of danger. With Him there are no incurable people. He set a man free from demons; a woman was healed from disease, and a child was delivered from death. Only the Great Physician could have made a difference in these three incidents.

Jesus' Power over Demons. 5:1-20

The story of the Demoniac of Gadara illustrates well the saying, "God forms a man; sin deforms a man; society informs a man, but only Christ can transform a man." On disembarking from the boat on the opposite shore of Galilee the morning after the storm, Jesus and His disciples were met on the towering headland by the lone figure of a wretched man. Broken chains hung from his wrists; his naked and gaunt body was covered with scars and bleeding sores. His hair was knotted with dirt and blood, and wild terror was seen in his deep sunken eyes. Leaping from rock to rock he came running down the barren hillside to where Jesus was and fell down at His feet to worship Him. Even as the man cried out Jesus commanded the unclean demons to leave him. Who was this man?

Satan tried to ruin him with demons. The root of the man's problem was the devil's work. His life had become the battle ground for demonic objectives. Demons are real, and at the time of our Lord, there was frantic demon activity. These demons declared their number as being Legion. Legion was the biggest unit of Roman soldiers and generally numbered six thousand. We do not know for how long this army of demons had trampled all over the man's life, but they were intent in destroying any vestige of sobriety and sanity.

The legions of hell are still intent in marring the image of God in men's lives.

In Recife, Brazil, on Friday, June 9, 1995, Geovane Soares, a 29 year old unemployed Satanist, was arrested and charged with violating corpses in the local cemetery. On the day he was arrested he had eaten the foot and leg of a three month old baby who had died the previous week. Geovane by his own admission was possesed with demons, and every three days he felt the compulsion to eat human flesh removed from the graves of the cemetery where he slept at night. On the following day here in Brazil, a Satanist group attacked a defenceless Jose Rodrigues Pinheiro with machetes and chopped him to death "just for the fun of it." Demon activity is not something unrelated to our times. All around us satanic activity is evident.

When Jesus commanded the demons to come out of this man, He called them in the singular because He knew them every one. He not only knew their number but also their nature, for he described them as "unclean demons." These filthy demons undoubtedly manifested their activity with foul profanities and lewd and unseemly behaviour. There is still much demon activity today, and much of the moral filth which permeates and pollutes our society is the result of demonic energy. However, not all demons necessarily express uncleanness. Satan sometimes appears as an angel of light. Satan worship is on the increase across the world and demonic groups are active in propagating their evil designs. These forces of darkness are all engaged in warfare in heavenly places against God and against His Son. This man was a sad and desolate specimen of the devil's work.

Society tried to reform him with chains. The Galilean region of Decapolis was made up of ten cities under Roman rule. The poor demonised man must have caused many disturbances in those cities. Children ran from him, and women were terrified of him. Perhaps at first the authorities tried to restrain him. Some might have tried to tame him, and others endeavoured to lock him in chains to rehabilitate him. He tore his clothes; he broke the chains; no man could solve his problems or stand his company. Unloved and unwanted, a menace to himself and the community, they finally made him an outcast on the hills of Gadara. He was separated from family and friends. Society could not help him. They saw him as a maniac. Jesus saw him as a man.

A sad insight was given to the twisted values of that society when Jesus cast the demons out of the man and sent them into a herd of two thousand pigs. In the city there was no great rejoicing for the deliverance of the demonised neighbour. They were too blind to recognise that this was the greatest thing which had ever happened in their community. Rather, they lamented the loss of the pigs and subsequently asked Jesus to leave their region. These hard hearted and small minded people had to learn that one individual life is worth more than a fortune in pork. It is sad when the community thinks more of sales than of souls—more of their produce than of the people. Where such values prevail there is little room for the Saviour.

The Saviour came to redeem him with great power. Society saw the wretch as a maniac; Satan had made him a demoniac, but Jesus saw him as a man. The Saviour came with the purpose to redeem this one man and change him. Six thousand demons could not withstand the Saviour. He stilled the raging sea and brought peace to a troubled heart. Not only was this man changed, Jesus commissioned him to go home and tell the family and neighbours what great things had been done for him. I like to picture this converted man returning to those cities with new clothes on his back, peace in his heart, a spring in his step and a song of praise on his tongue telling people the great things the Saviour had done for him. It must have been the talk of the town. Could it be that because of the influence of this one man's testimony that when Jesus came to the coasts of Decapolis later in His ministry, over four thousand people came to hear Him?

Jesus! the Name High over all,
In hell, or earth, or sky:
Angels and men before it fall,
And devils fear and fly.

Jesus' Power over disease. 5:25-34

Three boys had to give a definition of what faith is. One said, "Faith is taking hold of God." The second said, "Faith is holding on to God." The third said, "Faith is not letting go of God." Each boy was right.

This portion of Mark relates to us the story of a woman with an issue of blood. Had the unnamed lady in this miracle been asked her definition of faith, she might well have said, "Faith is touching Jesus." While multitudes thronged around the Saviour, only this pathetic woman in desperate need, reached out and touched Him. Her touch was the touch of faith which brought healing virtue from the Saviour.

The lady's hopeless plight. The case history of this lady would have made depressing reading. Her plight seemed hopeless. Physically she was drained of health. A debilitating disease had sapped her strength. In the pursuit of a cure she had been left financially destitute. Worse still, it seemed that she was socially isolated, and because of her disease she was religiously unacceptable and unclean. Try to imagine what it would have been like to be in her shoes. This woman's life was a misery.   No health, no help and no hope made her a woman to be pitied.

The Lord's heavenly might. The desperation of her plight led her to Christ. We are told by Mark that when she heard about Jesus, she pushed through the crowd from behind and touched Him. She had never heard the text, "Faith cometh by hearing and hearing by the Word of God." What she heard was mingled with faith, and that faith activated her hand to reach out to touch the Lord Jesus. That contact brought health to her body, help and peace to her soul and hope for her future. His power had transformed her plight from hopelessness to happiness and peace.

The miracles of the Lord Jesus are but reflections of our need of Him and what He can do in our lives. He still effects miracles in lives that have been marred. The lady's physical need exemplifies our condition without Christ. We are the helpless victims of our own sin. Many, in vain attempts to rid themselves of their sin, have tried the various doctors of the soul to no avail. Reformation and religion are but a few of the vain and futile remedies we try. Jesus Christ alone is the Great Physician. He can open eyes that have been blinded; He can change hearts that are hard; He can cleanse the guilty conscience and turn feet to the road of righteousness and heaven.

Jesus' Power over Death. 5:21-24; 35-43

In every incident in this chapter it is striking that each person who came to Christ did not come because of their admiration for Him. Their need compelled them to seek the Saviour. Our need is often the forerunner to grace. That was certainly the case in the home of Jairus.

The father's request. Jairus is the only person in the whole chapter who is identified by name. He was a well known official of the synagogue in Capernaum where Jesus attended. He probably made up part of the crowd when Jesus cured the man with the withered hand. It is amazing, and yet it is very human that we often solicit help from the Lord only when we are in dire need. What parent cannot identify with Jairus in his agony and anxiety as he saw the life of his little girl ebb away? He forsook his watch at his daughter's bedside; he forgot his high rank at the synagogue and disregarded the comments of the crowd and quickly rushed to the shore where he found Jesus. Reverently and unashamedly he bowed before the Lord and passionately he prayed the Lord to come with urgency and save the life of his dying daughter. This man had a conversion experience which was evidenced by his changed opinion about the Saviour.

The family report. While Jesus delayed to heal the diseased woman, crushing news came to Jairus from home. "Thy daughter is dead: why trouble thou the Master any further?" Jesus heard what was said and countered, "Be not afraid, keep on believing." Jairus had just witnessed the restoration of a woman who had been ill for twelve years. By this miracle Jesus gave him hope when all seemed hopeless. Jesus told him to have faith when fear seemed to be justified. The trial of our faith works patience, and patience works experience.

The final result. When Jesus arrived the little girl was ready for the cemetery, and the professional mourners had already gathered to chant their lament. He put out the scorners and the mourners and closed the door admitting only the distressed parents and the inner circle of three disciples. Peter must have told Mark how the Saviour lit up the home with His tender words of love and life as He raised the child back to life. Jairus had asked for restoration. The Saviour purposefully delayed His answer and brought more than restoration. He brought resurrection for even death could not obstruct His authority.

At a funeral our Lord raised a young man from the dead who had been in the vigour of youth. He raised a grown man from the dead in the cemetery. Here he raised a little girl in her own home. Each miracle was performed in the same way—He spoke to the dead. Dr. Vernon McGee explains that *talitha cumi* was an endearing expression in Aramaic. "Little lamb, wake up!" Two delighted parents were overjoyed as the little girl rose from the bed and became an active twelve year old again and found her appetite. What sounds of joy and sense of love must have filled that home.

Not danger, demons, disease nor death can oppose the command of our Sovereign Saviour.

CHAPTER ELEVEN

Jesus At Home And Abroad

MARK CHAPTER 6 VERSES 1-29

Over one hundred thirty years ago, Thomas Howard Payne was the American Consul General to Tunis. For Christmas he travelled across the Mediterranean and travelled on to visit Paris. On the evening of Christmas Eve he peered out the window of his hotel room on the busy crowds that thronged the Parisian streets. Thomas' thoughts turned to his family and loved ones back home in the USA, and he felt very lonely. In the heartless and desolate atmosphere of that hotel room he sat down and penned some famous words that were charged with emotion then and still are today for those who find themselves distant from their families and loved ones:

Mid pleasures and palaces, though far we may roam,
Be it ever so humble, there's no place like home.

"There is no place like home" was true for Jesus Christ during His earthly ministry but for all the wrong reasons. In no other place was He received with such doubt and disdain as in His own home town of Nazareth. In spite of their persistent rejection, the Saviour with loving patience and tender persistence, came back home again.

This second longest chapter of Mark's Gospel holds some of the saddest and darkest episodes in the life of our Lord. It is a chapter which is characterised by hardness of heart and unbelief both by family, friends, foes and even by His followers. The scepticism and unbelief of the Nazarenes bound the Saviour's hands so that He could do no mighty work. The scheming and conniving of a dancing damsel resulted in Herod taking the head off John the Baptist, and later, doubt and fear again gripped the hearts of the disciples in the face of what seemed to be insurmountable difficulties.

Jesus spoke at home. 6:1-6

From the wonderful events around the Sea of Galilee, Jesus took His disciples to His home town of Nazareth, but there was no red-carpet treatment waiting for the Greatest Citizen of this sleepy Galilean town.

Jesus returned home.

"He came unto His own and His own received Him not," said John the Apostle. (John 1:11) The rejection felt by Jesus Christ was never more painful than in His hometown of Nazareth. Of all people, the citizens of Nazareth should have known who Jesus Christ really was. The accounts of the visits of the Angel of the Lord to the town to announce the birth of the Messiah and the subsequent miraculous birth of the Saviour must have been talked about in the town. It was here that Jesus spent His childhood and His adolescent years as a carpenter in Joseph's work shop. Was there not something about Him that distinguished Him as He grew in grace and stature? It was also here in Nazareth that Jesus embarked on His public ministry on the day in the synagogue when He read the Scriptures from Isaiah 61:1, "The Spirit of the Lord is upon me." At first the people were filled with wonder at the gracious words He spoke, but they were soon filled with wrath and tried to push Him off a high mountain. More recently He had even been reproached by his friends and family who believed He was "beside Himself." (Mark 3:21)

Mark here registers yet another attempt by our Lord to reach out to the people of His own home town in spite of their repeated rejection. This long-suffering attitude was just like Him—patient yet persistent. He came back because there was still someone in the town who needed Him. Undoubtedly, these repeated visits were a factor in the later conversion of His own brothers, James and Jude, to whom He appeared after His resurrection.

The Jews resisted Jesus' honour. Jesus Christ said, "The prophet is not without honour, but in His own town." Although the prophet may be robbed of his honour, the prophet is still the prophet. Public opinion is not what makes the man. Public opinion in Nazareth was prejudiced against this Prophet who was like unto Moses.

The people of Nazareth were too near to see Him as He was. When they saw His works and heard His wisdom, they questioned, "Is not this the carpenter?" They were sceptical of how a carpenter could do such mighty works. When they heard His wisdom, they continued, "Is not this the son of Mary?" A Jewish son was remembered and respected because of his father's standing. When they referred to Him as a "son of Mary," it was a deliberate insult suggesting that the father of the child was unknown and questioning the integrity of the mother and the legitimacy of His birth. They poured derision on Him for not being the product of a rabbinical school. In almost the same breath they further belittled Him, "He is the brother of James." Someone has said, "An expert is an ordinary man who comes from another town." Jesus was robbed of honour in Nazareth because they were too near to see Him as He was.

The people of Nazareth were too blind to see Who He was. Unbelief caused spiritual blindness which robbed them of an appreciation of who Jesus was and of how much they needed Him. Gypsy Smith once said, "I never lost sight of Who Jesus Christ is and how much He loved me." Their blindness had robbed them of a recognition of His worth and of their own need.

The people of Nazareth were too proud to admit how great He was. "They were offended at Him." (Mark 6:3) Jesus had become a rock of offence upon which they stumbled, for they saw Him only as a carpenter and judged Him to be no greater than themselves. Pride is the sin that brought down Lucifer and is still the destruction of those who indulge in fiendish pride.

The Jews restricted Jesus' help. "And He could do there no mighty work... and He marvelled because of their unbelief." (Mark 6:5-6) Jesus Christ either marvels at our faith or at our unbelief. Matthew 8:10 relates how He marvelled at the faith of a humble centurion Gentile who had come from abroad. Now He marvelled at the faithlessness of the hard hearted Jews who had been His neighbours. I sometimes wonder if the Lord marvels at the behaviour of the saints today—their lack of faith, their sterile love and their lack of enthusiasm for the Lord.

Because He was unrecognised, Jesus Christ remained unhonoured in Nazareth. He was its greatest Son and bore the name of Nazareth to the cross.

Because of their unbelief, He who had been a carpenter in the town was unable to do any mighty work amongst them.

Because they limited His power, they, in turn, limited the blessings they received from His ministry. Unbelief was the greatest robber in Nazareth Unbelief had insulated them against the power of the Saviour. Jesus would have done mighty works but was not able to because unbelief tied the hands of omnipotence. I like the way Dr. Kent Hughes puts it, "Jesus *could* not do miracles because He *would* not. Omnipotence is not omnipotence if it is bound by anything but its own will. Jesus was morally compelled not to show His power. Unbelief freezes the exercise of God's power."

Jesus sent apostles away. 6:7-13.

When Jesus encountered disbelief in His home town He left with His disciples to preach in the small villages. There is a lovely story of Dr. C.I. Schofield who had been invited to preach in a certain church. On the night of the special meeting it rained very heavily, and only twenty people turned up. The embarrassed preacher apologised to Dr. Schofield for the small number who had come to hear his preaching and teaching. Dr. Schofield replied, "Young man, my Lord had only twelve men in His school and in His congregation most of the time. If He had only twelve, who is C.I. Schofield to be concerned about a big crowd?" I find that counting heads is a disturbing thing among preachers. Jesus Christ invested three years with twelve men—one of whom was a traitor.

Our Saviour had enlisted these men to be with Him that he might send them. They had been with Him in wonder and in woe, in public and in private, in confrontation with danger, demons, disease and death. They had seen faith honoured by mighty works, and their unbelief had been reproved by the way it limited the Holy One. They had truly been in the school of faith with Christ, and this must have heightened their sense of weakness and inadequacy. That was the very qualification they needed. To be sent by Him demanded faith to trust Him and fortitude to serve Him, for the way would not be easy. A friend of Hudson Taylor spoke to him about the founding of the China Inland Mission saying, "It must give you deep satisfaction to be chosen by God to start this vast enterprise." Mr. Taylor replied, "It seemed to me that God looked over the whole world to find a man who was weak enough to do His work, and when He at last found me, He said, 'He is weak enough - he'll do!' and so He sent me."

The only time the word "apostle" is used as a noun in Mark's Gospel is in chapter six verse thirty. "Apostle" refers to the office occupied by the twelve whom Jesus had chosen. However, the same word is used as a verb of the Lord Jesus when Mark wrote, "He began to send them." As an action word, *apostello* means "to send someone with special authority, on another's business, to accomplish his work." As such, an apostle was not his own; he represented Another.

They did not go at their own authority. They were especially commissioned by the Saviour.

They did not go to fulfil their own ambitions. They were under the control of the Saviour.

They dared not go in their own ability. They were given power from the Saviour.

When the mission was finally completed, they were fully accountable only to the One Who sent them.

It is interesting that the Saviour told the apostles to shake the dust from off their sandals where they were not well received. This was a custom observed by Jews as they travelled. When they had passed through a Gentile area, they would shake off the Gentile dust. Jesus taught His disciples to shake off the dust of the unbelieving Jews of the House of Israel. Their minimum provision which Jesus ordered them to take was designed to bring out the maximum faith in their journey. The Saviour still works through those who are weak enough to prove Him, willing enough to obey Him and simple enough to trust Him.

Jesus' fame spread abroad. 6:14-29

I remember as a student at the W. E. C. Missionary Training College in Glasgow old Brigadier General Frost used to lecture us, and on one occasion he said, "Boys, always remember wherever you preach throughout the world, a man's conscience is always on the side of the Gospel." Conscience is a detective that seeks to regulate our behaviour. It is our moral eye which is vigilant to reprove each thought, word or deed. Conscience is a God-given counsellor and guide in the heart of every man. It is always on the side of the Gospel.

The story of Herod Antipas is the story of the life and death of a conscience. He sinned against his conscience. Herod was a flamboyant lover of pleasure with little thought for morality, God or eternity; however, sharp-shooting John the Baptist had confronted him about his licentious living. For reasons both personal and political,

Herod put John into prison to try to silence the man who troubled his conscience.

As a birthday honour, Herod threw a banquet for the entertainment of his male friends. When the evening was in full swing, Salome, the daughter of Herod's lover, Herodias, danced to entertain the King. Gratified with Salome's charm, he roared, "Ask of me what you will, and I will give you up to half of my Kingdom." Inspired by her infamous mother, Salome asked for the head of John the Baptist on a platter. Conscience tore Herod apart as he was distressed. He complied with the girl's request and executed John. Herod's conscience was seared.

When he heard of Jesus Christ, Herod's conscience was stirred again. He believed John had been raised from the dead. Sadly the stirring of the conscience was not followed by repentance and faith in Christ. Later, Herod summoned Jesus Christ to his presence before He was crucified. The Saviour stood before him, but Jesus' voice was silent as was also Herod's conscience, and the immoral King was forever lost. John the Baptist lost his head but kept his conscience. Herod lost his conscience, and with it he lost his soul.

CHAPTER TWELVE

Does Jesus Care?

MARK CHAPTER 6 VERSES 30-56

Just a few weeks ago one of our missionary neighbours was killed in the Amazon, a victim of a tragic traffic accident. Bill McCoy and his wife were to fly home tonight for their first furlough after completing five years with New Tribes Mission. Instead, Bill's broken-hearted widow travelled home alone to meet her grieving children and share in their bereavement. It was grief such as this that caused the hymn writer to pen the words,

Does Jesus care when my heart is pained
Too deeply for mirth or song?

During this week you also may have asked one of these questions: "Is what is happening to me fair?" "Is God interested in my circumstances?" "Does Jesus care about how I feel and what I face?" If these or similar questions haunt your soul, then you have come to the right chapter of Mark's Gospel to find reassuring answers. Everything about the incidents which follow are eloquent affirmations that Jesus really does care.

Jesus cared for harassed servants and their work. 6:30-31

The disciples returned from their mission with great enthusiasm and excitement for all which they had witnessed and done. At the same time, the Saviour recognised their need for relaxation and renewal. For this reason, Jesus invited them to a deserted place away from the stir of the crowds and the flurry of activity. Why did Jesus invite His disciples to such a retreat? The folksy American preacher Vance Havner said, "If you don't come apart, you will come apart." Think about that. We have also heard it said, "The string that is kept tight is in danger of breaking." For the Christian, God's work is our delight and duty, but it is also demanding, and at times draining. These disciples were called upon to come aside:

To relax from the pressures of the work. Our Lord said, "He must work the work of the Father while it is day." Yet we find His humanity shining through when He slept on a ship, drank at a well and cooked fish by the sea. Engaging in Christian work is not only physically exacting, but often it is emotionally and spiritually draining. He knows our limitations. We all need time to relax.

To retreat from the pull of the world. God's people are not of the world, but they live in the world. When a boat is in the water it floats, but when water gets into the boat, it sinks. The Christian must be on his guard lest he is flooded by the tide of moral permissiveness and spiritual decadence that prevails today. We all need time to be refreshed.

To be renewed in the presence of the Lord. Have you ever been embarrassed and stranded because your car ran out of petrol? I have. I feel the same way when I lose out and am spiritually stranded only to find I failed to take time to be alone with the Lord. We cannot go far on a dry tank, an empty stomach or a barren soul. We all need time for renewal. He still invites us to spend time alone with Him.

Doing God's work is important. Being effective in God's work is paramount.

Jesus cared for hungry souls in the desert. 6:32-44

The feeding of the five thousand is one of the greatest miracles that Jesus ever did. Not only was the event recorded by all four

Gospel writers, but there were more than five thousand witnesses to the authenticity of the incident. There are many aspects of the story on which to major.

What Jesus saw. He saw the lateness of the hour, for He said the day was far spent; He saw the emptiness of the place, for it was deserted, and He saw the weakness of the people, for some were faint. He saw the pitiful people as sheep without a shepherd and had compassion on them. To the Shepherd, the sheep were both valuable and vulnerable. The Pharisees were not shepherds to the distressed people. Jesus came as the Good Shepherd and gave His life as a ransom for many.

What Jesus said. "Give ye them to eat." The disciples had come up with their answer to the problem of coping with the crowd. Some said send them away to buy their own bread. Philip suggested if the apostles had equal to a year's salary in their purse, they could feed such a multitude. But Jesus cut right through their human solutions and challenged them to minister to the crowd. The challenge to the church today is to feed the multitudes. Alas, we still come up with our lame excuses and human solutions to the global problem of reaching the masses with the Bread of Life.

What Jesus used. Andrew found a boy who had brought his five barley loaves and two small fishes. Barley bread was a poor man's picnic lunch. The rich lived off the finest wheat. The boy surrendered it all to Jesus, and the miracle of feeding the five thousand is the rest of the story. Jesus can use the poorest morsel yielded to Him. Hazel Miskimmin's literature witness in Manaus, Brazil, is the smallest stall at the central market. Some have labelled it as being inconspicuous in its missionary endeavour. However, through this one life yielded to Jesus Christ, God has used Hazel to reach hundreds with the Gospel. Wherever we go in the Amazon we find many people, both prosperous and derelicts of society, whom Hazel has led to Christ at the "inconspicuous witness" at the market. Little is much when God is in it!

Washington Cathedral was finally opened a few years ago after seventy years in construction. Back in the mid 1930s, the windows of the Cathedral were commissioned from a skilled glazier who lived in Huntingdon Valley, Pennsylvania. The glazier used a converted barn at the rear of his home as a workshop to prepare the stained glass windows. Those who commissioned the windows asked that scenes illustrate the life and ministry of Christ leading up to His death and resurrection. The glazier used members of his family and neighbours in Huntingdon Valley as role models of characters in the life of Christ.

When the glazier came to make the scene of the feeding of the five thousand, he used his friends and neighbours as faces in the crowd. However, when he looked for someone to pose as the boy who gave his two fishes and five loaves to the Lord, he felt he should use his own seven year old son. That decision proved to be almost prophetic, for twenty years later that same son, just like the boy in the miracle, gave his all to Jesus Christ to meet the needs of a hungry multitude.

The name of that glazier was Mr. Saint. Two of his children became missionaries in Ecuador. The name of his son was Nate Saint, the missionary pilot, who in February 1956 was martyred in Ecuador with four of his colleagues at the hands of the Auca Indians whom they gone to reach with the Gospel. Mr. Saint's other child was Rachel Saint who went on to complete a life-time of missionary service to the very Indians who had slain her brother. Like the boy in the miracle, they surrendered all they had to reach the tribes.

Two little fishes, five loaves of bread,
Tired, hungry people by Jesus were fed.
This is what happens when one little lad,
Gladly gave Jesus all that he had.

Jesus satisfied them all. "They all did eat and were filled." There was not just a little for each; they all received just what they needed and were filled. It is likely that many had not been filled or satisfied before.

Jesus surpassed their expectations. After the contented crowd had departed, the disciples picked up twelve baskets full of fragments that were left. Jesus Christ did far above their expectations and their wildest thoughts.

Jesus cared for helpless sailors at night. 6:45-54

A weather beaten sea captain was converted after being at sea for many years. A few days after his conversion he said to his pastor, "I'm going to sea tomorrow but never with so light a heart. I have been sailing for fifty years, and this is the first time the Great Pilot Jesus Christ has been with me, holding the wheel of my heart."

Mark related the story of another great storm on Galilee which brought the fear of death to Jesus' disciples. The Scriptures speak of many storms which were just as great as those on Galilee—storms of grief and guilt that assail heart and soul. In telling this incident in the life of the Lord, Mark lets us see some great parallel truths that are a comfort for us in the storms that strike us.

The storm was in His plan. Jesus constrained them to enter the ship then sent them to Bethsaida in the night. He knew the storm was coming. Quite often God's vehicle to accomplish His purpose for us is to let us pass through a storm. When John Wesley, yet unconverted, was returning from missionary service in America, God used a storm to show John that the Moravian Christians had something which he did not have. This, for John Wesley, was the start of a search which led to His conversion. John Newton, slave ship captain and drunkard, was converted through the means of a storm when he feared he would die.

While they journeyed, He prayed. Tossed by angry waves, alone they faced the height of a gale. Meanwhile, Jesus was face to face with His Father on high, praying for them. When Satan seeks to sift us or to swamp us, we have a Saviour praying for us and the Holy Spirit interceding for us.

When they were in peril, His presence was near. He came when they needed Him most—in the darkest and most dangerous hour of the night. He came the way they needed Him most—walking on the water. The storms could not swamp Him. He promised, "When you pass through the waters I will be with you." He never leaves us alone.

His peace filled their hearts. "Be of good cheer: It is I am." He is the great "I AM". He not only stilled the storm on the sea but also the storm in their hearts.

So I thank Him for the sunshine
And I thank Him for the showers,
I thank Him for the storms He brought me through,
For if I'd never had a problem,
I'd never know that God could solve them,
I'd never know what faith in God could do.

Through it all, through it all,
I've learned to trust in Jesus, I've learned to trust in God
Through it all, through it all,
I've learned to depend upon His Word.

Jesus cared for the hurting sufferers of various diseases. 6:55-56

The many who heard. As soon as Jesus arrived in Genneserat He was recognised, and word spread that Jesus had arrived. Those who were able-bodied filled the region with the news that Jesus was present. Perhaps they had been prompted by the news of what had happened to the woman who only touched the hem of His garment and had been made whole.

The many who hurt. Those who had gone running with the news of Jesus' arrival must also have returned carrying the sick, the lame and the needy to the Saviour. All of this is a challenge to us today. How blessed we would be if able bodied Christians would fill our communities with the news that Jesus is here and is able to change lives. If only we would seek out the needy and bring them all to the Saviour.

The many who were healed. While the helpers brought many to Christ, only those who reached out and touched Him were made whole. Those who were unwilling to reach out remained with their infirmity.

This chapter is an eloquent testimony to how much Jesus cares for all of us.

CHAPTER THIRTEEN

Hypocrisy Versus Reality

The developments of Jewish history during the Israelites' exile and eventual return to Israel, gave rise to many religious groups and various political alliances. Best known among these were the Scribes, the Pharisees, the Saducees and the Herodians. All of them felt that they were guardians of the Mosaic Law and protectors of the promised land. The Scribes were founded by Ezra and set up the use of synagogues for the reading and exposition of the Law; however, by the time our Lord had come, they had degenerated to be propagators of error by which they held to the traditions of the "Oral Law," that which tradition said was handed down from Moses but not written in the Scriptures. The Pharisees also had a worthy beginning in seeking to protect Judaism from foreign influence and infiltration. Their strict adherence to their interpretation of Old Testament law and their strong nationalist aspirations motivated them to try to establish a Messianic Kingdom on earth. The Saducees were the elite and liberal group of the time who dispensed of the supernatural factor in religion and had little regard for tradition. The Herodians were political activists who wanted to promote a Jewish kingdom under the rule of the Herods.

All these groups competed and contended with the others, but they formed an unlikely alliance in their opposition to the Saviour.

From the time of their inception until the crucifixion of our Lord, all of these groups played an increasingly active and vocal role.

When the general populace heard the Saviour, opinions were formed, and these opinions flowed in the two extremes of popularity and hostility. Some wanted to crown Him as King, while others planned to crucify Him. To the needy He was a hero, but with the religious legalists His rating was worse than zero. Early in this chapter our Saviour faces the religious group head on, toe to toe and eye to eye.

Jesus and the holding of traditions. 7:1-13

The externals of tradition. A special delegation of Pharisees and Scribes had been sent from headquarters in Jerusalem to further check out about this Galilean. With their biased minds and critical spirits, they censored and accused the disciples of our Lord for eating with unwashed hands. For the benefit of the non-Jewish readers, Mark explained some of the Jewish traditions which these groups held.

In this discourse Mark makes reference to tradition five times. Tradition played a big part in Jewish life then and still does today. There is nothing wrong with traditions in and of themselves providing the traditions do not oppose God's Word. However the Jews had created a system whereby they had countless laws and rituals which had taken the place of a personal and real relationship with God. They majored on that which had been passed down as the Oral Law, that which had come by word of mouth reputedly from the time of Moses. The observance of their traditions and esteem for the Oral Law had displaced their obedience to the written Word and made void the Law of God.

These traditions regulated national, social, religious and domestic life. If a Jew met a Gentile in a market place, he would have to go through a process of ritual cleansing after such Gentile contamination. It was even worse to meet a Samaritan! Utensils had to be washed or smashed; hands had to be cleansed and cups purified. This had nothing to do with hygiene. It was all an outward expression of their religion, yet it had no corresponding inner-experience of God.

The accusation against the disciples was that they ignored and disobeyed the traditions of the elders and neglected the ceremonial washings of hands and pots, etc.

An example of tradition. Jesus reprimanded their hypocrisy, highlighted one of the inconsistencies of these legalists and exposed their fraudulent behaviour. Moses in the Law had commanded both negatively and positively about the honour and welfare of parents. These legalists escaped their responsibilities by conveniently claiming the law of "Corban" and tried to circumvent the law of Moses. "Corban" was a vow which released a person from giving money for the support of parents if they dedicated the money as an offering to the temple. It seemed a worthy action, but the vow was never intended to be used to the neglect and disregard of parents. There was more prestige in giving to the temple; therefore these rascals indulged in religious trickery by dismissing their responsibility at home to gain prestige in society. Jesus said this was hypocrisy.

The effect of tradition. Deception and duplicity make a man an impostor. Jesus called them hypocrites. A hypocrite is just a play actor. He acts on the outside what he is not on the inside. A hypocrite is a person who pretends to be what he is not. Jesus Christ reserved His greatest condemnation for those who traffic in hypocritical religion. The Pharisees had worked a system of their own traditions and rituals and had substituted these external trappings of religion for a personal and experiential relationship with God. The outward form gave the appearance of godliness to these Jews, but inside they were empty. Jesus said they were whitewashed sepulchres.

Hypocrisy depends on outward ritual.   Truth offers inward reality.
Hypocrites try to keep traditions.   God's truth keeps us.
Hypocrites are slaves to traditions.   The truth sets us free.

It is easy to look at the Pharisees and other groups of that time and brand them for their hypocrisy, but there is a lot of hypocrisy in fundamentalist circles today. Some are only going through the ritual of giving consent to truth with little or no corresponding experience of God in their lives. We are in danger of being hypocrites when we pay more attention to our reputation than to our character. We are in peril of hypocrisy when we traffic in the external forms of our profession while our hearts are distant from the Saviour we profess to love. We indulge in hypocrisy when we major on virtues and fail to expose vices. There is nothing more obnoxious than fraudulent religion.

Jesus and the heart of our troubles. 7:14-23

Our Saviour gathered the people around Him and went to the root of the matter, "For from within, out of the heart of men, proceed evil thoughts, adulteries." (Mark 7:21) He pointed out the difference between external ritual and internal reality. By their empty formalism the Jews had focused on man's work and not on God. Outward religion pays attention to the fruit of sin, our sinful actions, but not to the root of sin which is the human heart. Our troubles are not physical; they are spiritual. Our need is not for external washings but for inner cleansing.

Henry Ward Beecher once said, "There are a hundred men hacking at the branches of evil for every one that is striking at the root." Governments constantly introduce new measures and spend millions trying to curb the rising wave of crime that afflicts modern society. Rehabilitation units are funded in an attempt to reform offenders. Legislation is introduced to protect our children from molesters. Various bodies are set up in a commendable endeavour to preserve marriages from coming apart. All of these measures are proper and necessary, but it is no good for society to chop at the fruits of evil when the problem is really at the root of the matter.

Jesus Christ continued to address Pharisees who were orientated to outward religion with emphasis on external washing, diets, etc.

The Saviour pointed out that a man's problem is not his stomach but in his heart.

Sin is not an error in behaviour, it is the enmity of the heart.
Sin is not a defect of environment, it is a disease of the heart.
Sin is not an accidental slip, it is the act of an enslaved heart.
Sin is not a pleasurable trifle, it is a tragedy of the heart.
Sin is not a man's blunder, it is the blindness of his heart.
Sin is not the weakness of a moment, it is the wickedness of a depraved heart.

Jesus Christ struck at the root of the matter. The Bible says: He was manifested to put away sin by the sacrifice of Himself. He bore our sins on His own body on the tree. He was made sin for us. The blood of Jesus Christ cleanses us from all sin. The blood of Jesus Christ goes to the root of the matter.

Jesus and our human tragedies. 7:24-30

In recent years the Queen's Birthday Honours List has been a matter of great debate as to who is really worthy of the honour and citations she confers. The Bible does not confer its commendations lightly. Of the thousands of named and unnamed people in the Bible, few had the distinction of being commended by the Saviour for their faith. More frequently, people were rebuked for their unbelief.

It is refreshing to read of this unlikely lady who showed exceptional faith in the Lord Jesus. He said of her, "O woman, great is thy faith."(Matthew 15:28) Mark reminds us that in the Gentile coastal territory of Phoenicia the Saviour could not be hid. It was here an unnamed woman in desperate need sought the Saviour and exercised great faith in Him. Why was her faith called "great faith?"

Her faith showed great concern for her daughter. This was a distraught mother, maybe a widow, breaking her heart for her little daughter. A demon held the girl tormenting her and obviously causing havoc in the home. Her need became a platform for faith.

Her faith conquered great difficulties in her way. There were many obstacles this woman had to overcome. She had the disadvantage of race, for she was a Canaanite. She had the disadvantage of being a woman. Only four of the thirty-eight miracles of Christ recorded in the Bible involve women. She had the disadvantage of location, for she lived outside Israel. Did her faith bring Christ to Tyre?

Her faith was confident in Jesus' great power. She was humble enough to take the place of a Gentile "dog" at Jesus' feet. Jews had rejected the mighty ministry of the Saviour, but this woman looked on His miracles as a mere crumb from the table.

Her faith was greatly commended by Jesus Christ. Exceptional faith brought an exceptional reward. The mother was rewarded, and the daughter was restored. Great faith sees God, and God sees great faith. Was it for her only that the Saviour stepped outside the bounds of His own land and His own people just to honour great faith?

Jesus and His hand of triumph. 7:31-39

Decapolis was not one city. The name means "ten cities." Recently we stood in the ruins of one of the ten cities just outside of Beit Shan. It was an area under Roman rule and had a lot of Gentile influence. Some commentators think that between the Gentile areas of Tyre and Decapolis our Lord spent eight months of His three year ministry. It was to this region the delivered demoniac had returned and told the great things the Lord had done for Him. Now another great miracle followed; by the touch of the Lord and the authority of His command, a deaf and dumb man received his speech and hearing. The first words he heard were from the voice of the Saviour. Although Jesus told him not to talk about it, the man could not keep quiet, and his first words were to tell everyone what the Lord had done for him. What songs of praise and shouts of joy must have been heard in those cities..

Mark sums up the work of Jehovah's Servant by this lovely commendation from the mouth of the people, "He hath done all things well." My Portuguese Bible states it even more beautifully, *"Tudo Ele tem feito esplendidamente bem:"*—"He has done all things splendidly well.." I say Amen to that.

CHAPTER FOURTEEN

It Is No Secret What God Can Do

MARK CHAPTER 8 VERSES 1-38

Some preachers earn the reputation of being long winded. A century ago it was not uncommon for a sermon to last for two or three hours, and even in Eastern Europe today long sermons still are in order. Many people have become conditioned sermon-tasters who expect a sermon to last no longer than twenty minutes. Such people seldom think that the fault is not so much with the long-winded preacher but with those who are short on hearing. At the beginning of chapter eight we find that not only did people flock in the thousands to hear the teaching and preaching of our Saviour, but they hung on His every word for three days. Now, that is long listening! They were so intent in listening that they missed their meals for those three days. Their rapt attention underlines the fact that no man spoke like this Man.

This chapter emphasises the busyness of our Lord doing His Father's business as He travelled by boat from place to place around Galilee and then on foot ascended into the modern day Golan Heights with his disciples.

Jesus responded to the distress of the multitudes. 8:1-9

Some readers confuse this miracle of feeding four thousand people with that of the previous miracle when Jesus fed five thousand people. Generally, when men tell a story, they augment and exaggerate the numbers, but on relating these happenings, Mark was careful to show that the figures were conservative and that this was a different miracle. This miracle happened at a different time, with a different number of loaves and with a different number of people in a different location. The first miracle happened at the north shore of Galilee, and this miracle occurred at the southern end of the lake. When the miracle was over, the disciples gathered a different measure of fragments that remained. The seven large baskets which held the fragments were larger than those used in the feeding of the five thousand, and they were the type used by Paul to escape from Damascus. (Acts 9:25)

Jesus' sympathy for the people. The Saviour ministered to the assembled people by His teaching and preaching, but He was not unaware of their physical needs. He noted many were far from home; they had fasted for three days, and as a result, many were at the pointing of fainting. Jesus said, "I have compassion on the multitude." Not only was He moved by their spiritual impoverishment, but the Lord had sympathy with their physical and social needs. The feeding of the five thousand seemed to have been exclusively for Jews. This provision for the four thousand was in the region of Decapolis, and the multitude may have included Jews but was predominately Gentile. He had mercy on Gentiles as well as on Jews. The Saviour refused to send them away hungry.

Jesus' supply of the provisions. He had satisfied their spiritual needs first with the Bread of Life, and He followed this by supplying bread for their bodies. As in the first feeding miracle, His supply again exceeded their need. The Lord does not limit His mercy according to our needs; He is able to do exceeding abundantly above all we ask or think. What the Lord did in Northern Galilee for Jews, He was also capable of doing for Gentiles in southern Galilee.

The American Country and Western singer, Stuart Hamblin, was converted to Jesus Christ in 1948. His life was so radically transformed that he wanted to return to his movie star friends in Hollywood and tell them what Jesus Christ had done in his life. He spoke to his close friend and mega-star John Wayne about the change the Saviour had made in his life, and he urged John to accept the Saviour also. John Wayne replied, "Stu, it's great what has happened to you, but it could never happen to a guy like me." Stuart Hamblin looked John Wayne in the eye and said, "John, it is no secret what God can do. What He's done for others He'll do for you." John Wayne knew how gifted Hamblin was with words and music and replied, "Stu, that sounds great. That line would make a great song." It did. Urged by John Wayne, Stuart Hamblin sat down and wrote the now famous hymn,

It is no secret what God can do.
What He's done for others, He'll do for you.
With arms wide open , He'll pardon you.
It is no secret what God can do.

Besides the people being filled and the disciples gathering seven baskets of crumbs that were left, Jesus' followers must have gleaned some lessons from that miracle. He taught them to love and sympathise with those to whom they minister. He instructed them as to the source of His power, for again He looked to heaven and blessed the bread. He showed them He was sufficient for every situation. Sadly, the disciples too soon forgot those lessons.

Jesus refused the demands of the Pharisees. 8:10-13

Mark immediately gives us a another contrast in the ministry of our Lord. Having met the need of the hungry crowd, Jesus left the area in a boat. He disembarked in Dalmanutha where He was confronted with the menacing Pharisees who pestered and tempted Him with fruitless questions.

The Pharisees demanded a sign from heaven. Beyond the demand, Mark highlighted the motive that was in their hearts, for they tempted Him. Argument is fruitless if it is motivated by prejudice and blindness. Every day the Saviour had been giving irrefutable signs, but they credited these to Beelzebub. They were not really interested in signs and much less interested in the Saviour. They attempted to trick the Saviour into making a mistake or to deviate from doing the Father's will. During the days of temptation Satan also asked for signs of Christ's deity. It was an impossible plot.

Jesus denied them with a sigh. The Saviour, moved with compassion for the needs of the crowds, now groaned, for He was hurt at the hardness of heart and unbelief of blind and prejudiced religious leaders.

Jesus departed from their shore. It was sad when Jesus Christ turned His back and departed. It was the Saviour's judgement on the Pharisees' continuing unbelief.

Jesus rebuked the dullness of His disciples. 8:14-21

There are fifteen questions asked in this chapter. In this portion of study Jesus Christ posed soul-searching questions to His disciples. Each question must have pierced the hearts of the Twelve. "Do you not understand? Is your heart still hard? Do you not see? Do you not hear? Do you not remember?" How could His disciples experience so many of Jesus' miracles and hear His words yet doubt Him? The answer to that question is found in ourselves, for often we doubt him too.

Did they forget the power of Christ to cast out legions of demons, to restore health to multitudes of people with diverse sicknesses, to raise a girl from the dead? Aleksander Solzhenitsyn said we should let our memory be our travel bag. In it we carry the luggage of life. "Lord, help me remember Your power when You saved me and raised me from spiritual death."

Did they forget the protection of Christ when He stilled the angry storm and hushed the raging waves on the Sea of Galilee? "Lord, help me remember how You graciously protected me from various dangers and snares."

Did they forget the provision of Christ when He turned water into wine, fed a multitude that exceeded five thousand people and did it again for over four thousand? "Lord, help me not forget how You provided for me in my times of need."

Did they forget the promises of power and authority which the Saviour gave them when He sent them out two by two? "Lord, please help me not forget the great and precious promises You have given in Your Word." The best place to keep your Bible is in your memory.

Jesus removed the darkness of a blind man. 8:22-26

Jesus performed another wonderful miracle near to Bethsaida, the home town of some of His disciples.

The manner Jesus employed. Jesus took the man by the hand and led him out of Bethsaida. This is the city which Jesus reproved for its unbelief, and perhaps like Nazareth, no great work could be done there. The man was not a native of Bethsaida for Jesus told the man not to return to the town.

The means Jesus engaged. The friends of the man had asked for Jesus to touch the blind man. Jesus applied saliva to the man's eyes and touched them with His hand. The blind man could not see Jesus, but the Saviour communicated with the man and encouraged His faith. There were seven blind men healed in the Gospels, and Jesus approached each one differently. He comes to us in just the way we need Him.

The miracle the man experienced. The amazing thing about this man's healing is that it was gradual. He passed through three stages. No sight, partial sight and perfect sight. It was the process this man needed. This is a picture of our experience in Christ. Once we also were spiritually blind. Now we see in part—through a glass darkly. When Jesus comes, we shall see Him face to face and see all things clearly.

Dr. Bill Woods is my colleague in Brazil. When we worked with Bill in Canutama thirty years ago he was so challenged by the blindness and deformities of many leprosy patients in the Amazon that he resigned from the Acre Gospel Mission in order to study medicine in Brazil. He graduated in medicine at the University of Amazonas and then specialised in ophthalmic surgery in Rio de Janeiro. He did further work alongside the well known Dr. Paul Brand in Carville, Louisiana, USA, where he learned the techniques of re-constructive surgery for deformed limbs. For the past twenty years Bill has been applying the gifts God has given him to treat the victims of leprosy, correct many of their deformities and give sight back to over five hundred people in the Amazon region.

I remember being with Bill one day when we met a lady he had not seen for some time. She nearly danced for joy to see him and was full of praise of him because she had been blind for nine years, and Bill had restored her sight. The lady's joy reminded me how this blind man and others of the New Testament must have felt when Jesus gave them back their sight.

CHAPTER FIFTEEN

Who Is Jesus Christ?

Who is Jesus Christ? This is a question which was frequently asked about our Saviour. It is a question which echoes as loudly today as it did when Jesus probed and penetrated the thinking of His disciples at Caesaria Philippi. It is a question we do not ask often enough, nor do we take enough time to answer. We never ask this question about any other notable person in the same way as we do about Jesus Christ, for there is no other person as majestic, as mysterious or as meaningful as the Saviour.

Caesaria Philipi was is on the lower slopes of Mount Hermon which today forms part of the Golan Heights. The location is known as Banias, and prior to the time of Christ it was called Paneas. This name was derived from the pagan worship that took place at the red rock cavern from out of which the bubbling waters pour and give rise to the River Jordan. To Jews it was the outer boundary of their region, for it was there that the Canaanites worshipped Baal and the Greeks erected a shrine in the grotto to their god, Pan. Herod Philip, son of Herod the Great, erected a white marble temple here to honour the deified Emperor Caesar Augustus. All this made Caesaria Philipi a conflict of false deities. Appropriately Jesus Christ posed the great question, "Who do you say that I am?"

Jesus revealed His identity and mission to His disciples. 8:27-33

Jesus Christ is the key Person to Mark's Gospel. What Jesus said and taught was of great importance. What Jesus did was of equally great importance. But Who Jesus Christ is is of supreme importance. At this point in time, He had been approved from heaven as God's Son and recognised by demons as the Holy One. To His disciples and to the people abroad He was Jesus of Nazareth. No one could understand who He was.

Who was Jesus Christ according to people's opinion? Some heard His preaching and teaching and concluded, as did Herod, that He was John the Baptist. Others witnessed His miracles and were sure He was Elijah. Still others were impressed with His compassion and saw in Him the weeping prophet Jeremiah. Public polls are never a good guide to what the truth is. People often form opinions without convictions, and error always has many voices. Truth has only one voice.

To many today He is a great human Teacher, the Carpenter of Nazareth, the Founder of Christianity, a Jew Who claimed to be the Messiah, a Martyr Who died for a noble cause. All of these claims are laudable, but all of them are flawed. The important thing is not what others think or say, but what the Scriptures say. The decisions of the crowd cannot be a substitute for your personal decision about the Saviour.

Who was Jesus Christ according to Peter's confession? Peter has often been blamed for saying the wrong thing. However, here he spoke with courage and conviction as he openly confessed, "Thou art the Christ the Son of the living God." Peter's response was not formed by public opinion but was based on the revelation that God the Father had given him. This contrasts greatly from earlier in the chapter when Jesus Christ indicated the blindness of the disciples. (8:18)

Who is Jesus Christ according to His personal admission? When the disciples understood and acknowledged He was the Christ, the Saviour then spoke about the cross and the purpose for which He came.

"The Son of Man must suffer many things..." This is the obedience of Jesus Christ to the Father's will.

"...must be rejected..." This is the opposition to Jesus Christ as predicted by the prophet Isaiah.

"...and be killed..." This is the offering of Jesus Christ on the cross. He spoke of a violent death at the hands of wicked men, yet there was a voluntary nature to His death also.

"...after three days rise again." Jesus overcame death by the resurrection.

Three times the Lord Jesus revealed to His disciples details of His coming passion, and on each occasion they failed to understand how the Messiah must suffer. Peter, who made the confession as to the Person of Christ, soon made a confrontation against Christ and His passion. Not only did Peter not understand, he probably did not really listen to hear the end of the statement. He was effectively saying, "No cross if you are the Christ." Satan was always opposed to the way and the work of the cross; Jesus Christ recognised his tricks and commanded, "Get you behind me Satan."

Who is Jesus Christ according to your personal confession? Although Peter is the one who responded, each of the disciples were asked the same question, "Who do you say that I am?" Each must give His own answer. Boiled down to basics, the essence, value and future of your life can all be distilled in the answer to this one important question our Saviour asked, "Whom do you say that I am?"

Jesus required devotion from His disciples. 8:34-38

Since there had been confusion as to the Person and passion of our Lord, there most certainly must have been ambiguity with regard to being a disciple of Jesus Christ. The Saviour spelled out the terms and the demands of discipleship. The disciple is not greater than his Lord. In the principles of discipleship as laid down by Jesus Christ, there is a portrait of the Saviour Himself.

A disciple is one who forsakes and forgets His own will. The denial of self is not easy, but it is the first step and then a pattern for life. It is the crucifixion of the self-life. The follower of Jesus Christ must learn to deny himself with the same strength that Peter denied His Lord.

A disciple is one who fulfils the Fathers will. The Father's will was ever uppermost in the mind of Jesus Christ, and the will of God for Jesus Christ led to the cross of Calvary. Cross-bearing for the Christian is doing what Jesus did—He did the Father's will. A surrendered will is an imperative for a disciple of Jesus Christ. Dr. Wilbur Chapman, the famed American evangelist, asked General William Booth the secret of his evangelistic success. The old General replied, "I will tell you the secret. God has had all there is of me to have—all the adoration of my heart, all the power of my will and all the influence of my life." That is precisely what God looks for in a disciple.

A disciple is one who follows Christ wherever He leads. The disciples learned this process, and it did not come easily. Soon they left Him and were scattered. All but Judas returned to follow Him until death. This pattern for discipleship has not been revoked.

I recall a story I heard some time ago of a man who had a dream.

I dreamt I visited the Celestial City and stood amongst the great multitude of the redeemed that no man could number. Next to me was a saint who had been in heaven for over 1900 years. "Who are you?" I asked. "I am a Roman Christian," He replied. "I was converted through the witness of Paul when he was a prisoner at Rome. I was persecuted for my faith and died in Nero's persecution of the Christians. They covered me in black pitch and fastened me to a stake. They then set me alight in Nero's garden." I was shocked. "That must have been terrible," I replied. "No, no," he responded, "I was glad to suffer for Him who died for me."

On my other side stood another one of the blood washed company. "How long have you been here?" I asked. "I have only been in heaven a few hundred years. I was won to Christ in the South Sea Islands when the missionaries came and told me about Jesus. After my conversion my own people caught me, beat me and clubbed me to death. They cooked me and ate my body." I was horrified. "How awful!" I exclaimed. "No, no," he replied, "I was glad to die as a Christian. I had been taught how Jesus was crowned with thorns and beaten for me." He then turned to me and asked, "And how did you suffer for Jesus Christ, and how much did you do for Him?" It was just then I was startled from my deep sleep and turned over in my nice soft bed.

Jesus Christ concludes His discourse on discipleship by showing the alternative life style to that of a disciple. To indulge in the self-life is to lose the life. To gain the world only is a bad investment. To be ashamed of Christ now will result in being ashamed to meet Him when He comes.

When Sir Francis Drake sailed the seven seas, he had in his crew a man from a village in Devon. One day the sailor was on shore leave in his village and met an old friend who had chosen to stay at home rather than sail with Drake. The landlubber pitied the sailor and said, "You have not made much out of these years." "No," replied the sailor, "I've not made much. I have been cold, hungry, shipwrecked, often desperately frightened, but I've sailed with the greatest captain that ever sailed the seas." Discipleship is the greatest investment and adventure we can know.

CHAPTER SIXTEEN

The Shining Son

My earliest recollection of my wife Audrey is that when I first met her she was always carrying a massive book that must have weighed more than two pounds. It was a copy of James Hudson Taylor's biography "The Growth of a Soul - Volume 1". As she travelled back and forth to work and to church by bus, Audrey ploughed her way through this challenging book. "The Growth of a Soul" was an appropriate title for the life of the founder of the China Inland Mission. From his early and weak beginnings in Yorkshire and the days of ill health in London, this remarkable man proved the heights and depths of the life of faith as he followed His Lord. Once in Australia he was introduced as "our illustrious guest" to which he replied, "Dear friends, I am the little servant of an illustrious Master."

Spiritual growth is never instant, even with the very best teacher and teaching. At the time of which this portion of Mark was written, the disciples had been with the Lord for over two years. They had gained experience with Him in cities and in villages, on mountain tops and on stormy seas, confronting demons and comforting the distressed. It all had been an education, and they were growing in the knowledge of the Lord. However, since the Saviour had begun to speak of His future suffering, death and resurrection, the disciples found it difficult to understand where it was leading them. Jesus allowed the inner three disciples, Peter, James and John, to join Him on the summit of a high mountain where they experienced something they would never forget and which would greatly add to the growth of their souls. Later Peter wrote, "We were eye witnesses of His majesty, for He received from God the Father honour and glory, when there came such a voice to Him from the excellent glory, 'This is my beloved Son in whom I am well pleased.' And this voice which came from heaven we heard, when we were with Him in the holy mount." (2 Peter 1:16-18)

The glory of Christ on the mountain. 9:1-13

From the lofty height of the mountain Jesus brought His followers down to the valley of reality where a heavy-hearted father was searching for someone to help his demon possessed boy. Furthermore, inept disciples disputed the finer points of theology and argued amongst themselves who would be the greatest in the Kingdom of God. There was a lot of growing to be done in this chapter.

Mark undoubtedly gleaned the details of the transfiguration from Peter who had vivid recollections of the events of that unforgettable day. It is interesting that in giving details of the transfiguration of the Lord, each writer of the synoptic Gospels gave a different aspect of the happenings on the holy mount. Matthew, who viewed Christ as the King, emphasised the countenance of the Lord as shining like the sun, and gave a parallel of John's vision of the Saviour in Revelation 1. Luke, who displayed the sufferings of Christ the sinless Man, majored on the topic of the conversation about the forthcoming death of Christ. Mark, who portrayed Christ as the active and able Servant of Jehovah, showed He had garments that were whiter and brighter than anything imaginable on earth. This was a glimpse of the Lord from glory. "His garments became shining and exceeding white as snow as no fuller on earth can white them." A "fuller" was simply a launderer or a bleacher who dyed the garments.

The garments of Christ are a study in themselves. One evening in 1915, Dr. Wilbur Chapman was preaching at the Montreat Bible

Conference, North Carolina on Psalm 45:8, "All thy garments smell of myrrh, and aloes and cassia, out of the ivory palaces, whereby they have made thee glad." Dr. Chapman developed a message on the beauty of the Person of Christ. On the way home from the meeting that evening a young British pianist, Henry Barraclough, wrote out some lines based on the thoughts of the message that night. The following morning the new hymn was sung as a duet at the Bible Conference.

My Lord has garments so wondrous fine
And myrrh their texture fills;
In fragrance it reached to this heart of mine,
With joy my being thrills

In garments glorious he will come
To open wide the door
And I shall enter my heavenly home,
To dwell forevermore,

On the Mount of Transfiguration took place the greatest conference of history. Two visitors from heaven were there, Moses as testimony of the Law, and Elijah as representative of the Prophets. The countenance and clothing of the Saviour shone with the inner glory of the Lord Jesus. The Father's voice was heard. Galilean fishermen were present and felt so good about it they did not know what to say. There was much to learn at this meeting on the mountain. They learned that Jesus was the Lord of glory as He shone in His brightness. They also learned that the saints in heaven share in the glory of their Lord and that He maintains communion with both those in heaven and those on earth. They further learned that saints in glory of different ages are instantly recognisable. Alas, in the midst of this experience they were overcome by the occasion and soon fell asleep.

On the Mount of Transfiguration took place the greatest conversation of history. They talked about the Saviour's exodus—His departure. Moses had led an exodus out of Egypt after the sacrifice of the pascal lamb which was a foreshadow of Jesus Christ, God's Lamb. Elijah had a personal exodus from earth to heaven when he was caught up to heaven, and this was a likeness to the foretold resurrection of Jesus Christ. Both of these men knew what they were talking about. The Law and the Prophets had long pointed to the coming Messiah. Now He would make His exodus through the death of the cross and rise again to pass into the heavens. Just a week previously Peter could not tolerate hearing of the Saviour's death, but he discovered that the death of Christ was the greatest theme of heaven.

On the Mount of Transfiguration was a great contrast to Calvary.

Mount Hermon was the mount of glory—Calvary was the place of grief.

Here was the outshining of His light—At Calvary was the outpouring of His life.

Here His clothing did not hide His glory— At Calvary clothing did not cover His shame.

Here Jesus stood between two worthies of history.—At Calvary He was crucified between two thieves of infamy.

Here His brightness outshone the sun.—At Calvary the darkness hid the sun.

Here was heard the Father's voice of approval from heaven.—At Calvary was heard the Son's cry of abandonment from earth.

Mark gave great details of the disciples reaction to the transfiguration. Peter addressed the Saviour, "Rabbi, it is good for us to be here." He wanted to erect three tabernacles, one each for Jesus and the two visitors from heaven. He wanted to put Jesus on equal par with Moses and Elijah and wished to remain on the mountain of glory and bypass the suffering of which the Saviour had spoken. It was then they were enveloped in a cloud out from which they heard the affirming voice from heaven, "This is my beloved Son, hear Him." When they lifted their eyes again they saw no one but Jesus. God had taken the patriarch and prophet back to heaven and focused the disciples' vision on Jesus exclusively.

The gloom of the Christless in the Valley. 9:15-29

Although we may be overwhelmed by the joys and glories of the Saviour on the heavenly mount, we must never forget the woes and overwhelming needs in the valleys of life. Dr. Kent Hughes gives a telling illustration of the transition from the mountain to the valley. "Raphael was one of the great masters of art. He literally died painting, for his last great painting was left unfinished. It was entitled, "The Transfiguration." The uppermost part of the painting showed the transfigured Christ on the top of the mountain with Moses and Elijah; lower, the three disciples, Peter, James and John, shielded their eyes from the blinding light. The bottom part of the painting depicted the valley where a demon possessed boy was surrounded by his distraught father and the other faithless disciples. This was Raphael's unfinished work." There is a lot of unfinished work to be done in the valleys of life.

The believer's position is in Christ and seated with Him in the heavenlies. However, our feet are on the ground, and we are passing through the "Valley of Bacca", the valley of bitterness and tears. As in the story Mark related, there are many boys and girls all around us who are oppressed by sin and Satan. The devil's intent is still the same today—to destroy their lives. Tragically, as in this story, we still encounter helpless servants of Christ who are incompetent because of their lack of faith. Like the ineffective disciples, we often substitute spiritual power with futile debate and discussion. We are so taken up in splitting hairs on non-essential and elementary matters that we neglect the vital role of an effective ministry to the masses who are held in the lap of the evil one and trapped in the valley of despair.

Satan cast the boy down. The boy was a pathetic spectacle. A demon seized him. Demons are not imaginary beings. They are real and are the emissaries of the devil to destroy lives. This foul demon made the boy scream, grind his teeth and foam at the mouth. He often fell into fire and water; and even worse, the demon had struck him deaf and dumb so that the boy could not even verbalise his need. It was Satan's design to destroy this boy, and he still strives to destroy our children.

The disciples let the boy down. "I spoke to thy disciples that they would cast him out; and they could not." The boy's father was greatly disappointed with the disciples. Without the Saviour, they could do nothing. The disciples had no vision of what Jesus could do. They had no faith in the power that Jesus had given them. Added to this, there was no prayer for the boy nor sense of urgency for his condition. The Saviour taught them afterwards that power to expel demons in this way comes only by prayer. The same is to be said of the church today; without Christ we, can do nothing. We need to catch the vision of our Saviour in glory which will equal the need of life's valleys. We need to engage in prayer and exercise the authority of the Saviour's name at this urgent hour.

The Saviour lifted the boy. Jesus came down from the mountain to rescue both the embarrassed disciples and the demon possessed boy. The father, who had been disappointed in the disciples, now doubted the Saviour. He questioned if Jesus was able to do anything. It was not the Saviour's ability that needed to be called into question; it was the ability of the man to believe. The father prayed for faith in spite of his unbelief. Jesus spoke to his disciples about their unbelief. He spoke to the father about his faith. He commanded the foul demon to depart. We do not read that He spoke to the boy. His action spoke louder than words. "And Jesus took him by the hand and lifted him up, and he arose."

True greatness for those who are climbing. 9:30-50

Jesus again was alone with the Twelve. On the road down from the Golans to Galilee and in the house in Capernaum, probably

Mark's way of speaking of Simon Peter's house, He spoke to them about essentials for their growth and development.

The certainty of His sacrifice. He taught His disciples and said unto them, "The Son of man is delivered." This is the second of three occasions when the Saviour predicted His suffering and sacrifice and always with the promise of the resurrection. Like dull students, they did not understand the lesson, and after Peter's rebuke, they were afraid of their own ignorance or even of suffering the same death. Our Saviour did not flee from the cross; the cross was the purpose for which He came.

The sincerity of true service. The disciples should have been ashamed of their behaviour, for while the Saviour spoke of His death, the disciples disputed who would be the greatest among them. Seeking the first place was common amongst the Pharisees. It may well have been that the three who ascended the holy mountain felt they had an advantage above the others. The Saviour exposed their private struggle and tenderly took a little child in His arms and taught them that the secret of greatness is servanthood. This is a lesson that the Saviour repeated many times, and even prior to His crucifixion the sense of rivalry was so great amongst the disciples that the only one who took the place of a servant was the Saviour with a basin and a towel.

The severity of all sin. With the child still in His arms, the gentle Saviour spoke of sin and hell in a radical way. No one preached more about sin and hell than Jesus Christ. He said it would be better to eliminate hand, foot or eye than to persist in sin and be in danger of hell.

Dr. Wilbur Chapman told the story of a minister who preached with great power against sin. He openly and penetratingly spoke of sin as "the abominable thing that God hates." One day a member of his church went to the minister's office and complained to him, "We don't want you to speak so openly about sin. Our sons and daughters are hearing so much about this that they will want to experiment with sin. Speak about the errors of life if you like, but don't talk to us so much about sin."

The minister went to the shelf of the medicine cupboard and brought down a little bottle that was marked **POISON**. "Please look at what you are asking me to do. I don't like the word poison so I am going to change the label to make it look like something that is more pleasant. Let's call it Peppermint. Now can you imagine what might happen? The more acceptable we make the label the more perilous is the poison. Let's call sin by it's name. It is an abomination in the sight of God."

CHAPTER SEVENTEEN

All In The Family

MARK CHAPTER 10 VERSES 1-52

Happy Families is not just a child's card game or a television show. It is God's plan for what the family home should be. Sadly, many have forgotten the Architect and His design for the home and have followed their own plans. The so called "alternative life-style" which by passes marriage can admit multiple partners and produces children outside the security and sanctity of the marriage bond. The results have been disastrous. In the United Kingdom the rate of divorce more than doubled between 1971 (74,000) and 1988 (152,000). Each year in our British society 150,000 parents with children under the age of sixteen divorce. The quick divorce which often negates opportunity for counselling and reconciliation, creates significant suffering and hardship, not only for the partners involved, but especially for the children of the broken relationship.

The effect of the disintegration of family life is obvious in society. The lack of respect for human life and law touches everything from school to industry to our homes. Currently 180,000 abortions take place in the United Kingdom each year; less than two percent are because of handicap or rape. It is blatant social murder which has been legitimised by the government which is also under pressure to follow to the next logical but immoral step of mercy killing the terminally ill. Pornography, which is worth more than £ 100,000,000 in the British Isles each year, is found in books, newspapers, magazines, comics, films, videos, television, telephone chatlines and even on computer software.

Is it any wonder that in the United States a leading psychologist declared, "The family as we know it is nearly at the point of extinction." Another leading psychiatrist said, "Family life is cracking at the seams, and an effective mortar is nowhere to be found." We may not share such pessimism, but we do not deny that the family is under attack. If the breakdown of family life continues at the same momentum as in the last generation, one fears to imagine how it will be for our children and grandchildren in years to come.

We should remember however, that family problems are not new. Jesus Christ addressed the question of marriage, children and adolescence when He was on His way to Jerusalem for the last time. He still addresses those problems today.

The question of marriage and divorce. 10:1-12

Like baying hounds the Pharisees pursued the Saviour in a vain attempt to trap Him. They questioned Him about divorce, not because they required an answer, they had already formulated their own opinions, but in order to trick the Saviour. Divorce was just as much a hot potato then as it is today. John the Baptist had lost his head because he dared to speak out against Herod for divorcing his wife and committing adultery with his brother's wife. The Pharisees obviously calculated that if Jesus spoke against divorce, it would appear He not only contradicted Moses, but would also set him at variance with Herod. If He approved of divorce, they would have accused Him of lowering His standards.

The Saviour was a master at countering the trick questions of the Pharisees, and as on other occasions, He came back at them with another question, "What did Moses command you?" This question took them back to the Scriptures where Moses permitted divorce. (Deuteronomy 24:1-2) From that Scripture the Saviour turned the discussion from one on divorce and laid down the original plan for marriage which still contains God's formula for a lasting relationship. Today we have many who are seeking justification from the Scriptures for divorce when the real issue which should engage their pursuit is that of making their marriage last. Divorce was not in God's original plan. Note the following from the teaching of the Saviour.

God's plan stresses the severance of family ties. "For this cause shall a man leave his father and mother." The marriage bond is the strongest and closest bond known in the human family. Sons and daughters were designed to eventually leave the family and be joined to another. In marriage all other ties are to be loosed to allow for a lasting relationship. Until we are joined in marriage we are members of one family with particular responsibilities and loyalties. At marriage we sever some of those ties, and with our spouse we become a separate unit.

God's plan focuses on the importance of loving commitment. Falling in love is a wonderful experience which stirs our emotions. Staying in love takes more than emotion. Love in the Scriptures is an act of the will. In the vows at the marriage ceremony the couple pledge their "I will" to each other. Many who say, "I don't love him any more," have simply lost the will to love. It has been said that our *will* is often in conflict with our *won't*. The "I will" of the marriage vow often becomes the victim of the "I won't" of convenience. It is better to make your emotions a prisoner of your will than to hold your will as a ransom to your emotions.

God's plan emphasises an acceptance of each other. "And they shall be one flesh." When God provided Eve for Adam she was designed as his help meet, his auxiliary, without whom he was incomplete. Mutual acceptance is important for a couple to adjust to each other. As they fulfil their roles in marriage they compliment and supplement each other. They are two people bound in one union.

God's plan insists on the permanence of the marriage bond. "What therefore God hath joined together, let not man put asunder." The marriage bond is "glued" by God. However, a man and a woman must work at making sure they stick together. Divorce was not in God's plan. The best marriage ring is really a triangle: a man, a woman and God. If you have a happy and lasting marriage, you ought to be grateful to God, for it is becoming a rare commodity.

Jesus' blessing on children. 10:13-16

"And they brought young children to Him." Following marriage many couples embark on the next logical step. This step will have a greater impact on them than the friends they have made, the jobs they pursue or the government they elect. Furthermore, the effect of this step will be felt for generations to come. What is this profound effect? They will have children. The arrival of children in a home is one of the greatest life-changing experiences. Ask any parent and especially those who have just had their first child.

Bearing, rearing, clothing, feeding, and educating children is costlier now than it has ever been. Added to this, in our secularised and polluted society the responsibility of instructing our children has never been greater. The most important things our children need in life cannot be bought with money. Like the mothers mentioned in the above text, we all need to bring our children to the Saviour. You cannot read the Bible without being impressed by our Lord's popularity with children. It tells us a lot about our Lord. It also tells us a lot about children.

Consider the mothers who brought their children. Had they read how Isaac, Moses, David and other great men, were all brought to God as children? Parents are not only their children's first teachers, they are their children's most effective teachers. This principle holds good for teaching the truth or teaching which is false. It is never too early to bring our children to the Lord in prayer and teach them the Scriptures. Happy is the child who, like Timothy, was taught the Scriptures from his infancy.

Consider the men who blocked the children. Sadly, the disciples became obstacles to these anxious mothers when they really should have been helpers. Did they so soon forget the lesson the Saviour taught when He took a child in His arms and said, "Whosoever shall offend one of these little ones that believe in me, it is better for him that a millstone were hanged about his neck and he was cast into the sea." (Mark 9:42) Perhaps their reasons seemed legitimate, but they displeased the Lord. It is difficult enough for children in our modern extravagant society, but it is sad when believers become an obstruction to children coming to the Saviour. Sometimes we are too blind to see the need of children and too busy to offer them help.

Consider the Master who blessed the children. What a beautiful word picture is painted for us when the Bible says, "He took them up in His arms, put His hands upon them and blessed them." His arms were outstretched to embrace them, His hands to touch them and His heart to bless them. Jesus Christ is the same today. Children need not and should not wait until they become adults before they come to the Saviour.

The Truth for youth. 10:17-31

"And Jesus beholding him loved him and said unto him 'One thing thou lackest." In the allotted span of seventy years, no other tenth of that span is more difficult, traumatic, exciting or enjoyable than the years we call our teens. These are the "becoming years." In them we emerge out of childhood to enter into the adult world. We fool ourselves when we think we live in an adult world. It is a teenagers' world. Teenagers set the fashions; they coin new words; they popularise music and often are the champions of our times. If life were like a soccer game, then it is youth that is on the playing field; children are on the subs bench and adults are the spectators!

During these exciting teenage years we wrestle with many questions and often grasp in vain for the right answers. In a search for identity we ask, "Who am I?" With a sense of responsibility we ponder, "Why am I here?" Even with a crisis of confidence we might ask, "What and where is my future?"

All of these questions seem to have been filling the heart and mind of this young man who came running to Jesus Christ in the pursuit of eternal life. This life is something he did not have and something he could not buy. The fact that he ran to Jesus Christ suggests not only his desire for real life, but also his disillusionment with the life he was living. His had been a life characterised by riches, religion, being a ruler and having a good education. Early he discovered that none of these could fill the emptiness of his heart or satisfy his soul.

Here was a lad who was very rich yet ended up very poor. He was so right in what he said yet so wrong in what he did. He was so good in the eyes of men, yet he was as bad as all other men. He was so near to finding life in the Saviour, yet he was so distant for he preferred his own possessions. He had been so wise to come to Christ, yet so foolish to reject the Saviour who loved him. What a man wants often differs from what he needs. The young man embraced his riches and neglected the One he needed most.

The Model for servants. 10:32-45

"The Son of man shall be delivered unto the chief priests and scribes and they shall condemn Him to death... for even the Son of Man came not to be ministered unto, but to minister, and to give His life a ransom for many."   Mark draws attention to the recurring prediction of our Lord about His coming death which stands in stark contrast to the ongoing discussion of greatness and position among the disciples.

When Oliver Cromwell was short of gold for coinage at the Royal Mint, he ordered his troops to round up all the ornate images of various saints from church pedestals. He then gave this order, "Melt the saints and put them into circulation." Often we put the Lord's disciples on pedestals as men devoid of a shred of selfishness. How wrong we are. They were human just like us. Jesus Christ was quick to challenge them to be rid of their selfishness and to melt them and mould them for discipleship.

Consider the selfish petition. When our Lord spoke about His passion and death at Jerusalem, Salome's two sons, James and John, asked Him to grant their desire and give them seats of prominence in His Kingdom. Their request was for what they wanted rather than what God willed. Selfishness is like that. It over-estimates self-importance and under- estimates the importance of others. Their request incensed the other disciples and caused sharp division.

Observe the sacrificial pattern. Living an unselfish life is an art called discipleship. Roman society was made up of position and prestige. Emperors had crowns; governors had palaces; generals had armies, and soldiers had medals. A slave was considered to be at the bottom of the heap. Jesus Christ dignified servanthood by indicating that He also was a Servant. By His life and death He elevated service and sacrifice to its rightful place. We are most like the Saviour when we are prepared to give and serve as He did.

Ponder the Saviour's prediction. Our Saviour courageously and confidently foretold His betrayal at Gethsemene, the mocking at the hands of the Jews, His scourging, spitting and crucifixion by the Romans and His resurrection on the third day. Jesus Christ not only had courage, but He was also in control of these events. The Saviour's passion is our pattern.

Mercy for a blind beggar. 10:46-52

When Jesus Christ passed through Jericho, at least two people were converted. The first was Bartimaeus who was probably the poorest man in town. He was a blind beggar who sat in the way as pilgrims made their pilgrimage to Jerusalem. The second convert was Zachaeus who was probably the richest man in town. He came to the Saviour from the sycamore tree and took Jesus Christ home.

A missionary who spent his life serving the Lord in the South Sea Islands died and was buried by the people whom he had won for Christ. At his burial place they erected a headstone on which these words were written, "When he came there was no light. When he left there was no darkness." This testimony sums up the experience blind Bartimaeus had of Jesus Christ. As soon as he received his sight, he followed Jesus." (Mark 10:52) All his life he had sat in darkness until he met Jesus Christ, the Light of the World.

Blind Bartimaeus had good vision. It seems he was blind from birth. That day he took his place at the old familiar spot in a forlorn hope that the passing pilgrims might toss him a coin. People spoke of Jesus of Nazareth passing by. What he heard was mingled with faith, and out of a needy heart he repeatedly cried, "Thou Son of David have mercy on me." Although he was blind, he could see his need. Although he was blind he recognised that Jesus was the Messiah and King. The worst blindness of all is spiritual blindness.

The beggar Bartimaeus found great treasure. All his life he had known nothing but begging. He had been living on the scraps and leftovers of other people. That day was different. Jesus said, "What will you that I do for you." Jesus Christ had opened the treasures of heaven to Bartimaeus. He asked for what he needed most—his sight. Normally beggars had nothing to give away, but as soon as he received his sight he threw away the beggar's garment. He did not need it anymore. He received something that money could not buy, and he received Jesus Christ as well. For Bartimaeus, throwing away the cloak was an act of faith; the word Jesus spoke to him was the assurance of faith; following after Christ was the adoration of that faith.

The believing Bartimaeus exchanged Jericho for Jesus. When he was miraculously healed he did not follow the crowd. He did not return to Jericho. The first face he saw was the face of the Saviour. The first thing he did was follow the Messiah. The road ahead led to the cross and shame, but Bartimaeus followed all the way, and he probably saw his Saviour on the cross. What a sight for a man who had been born blind!

CHAPTER EIGHTEEN

The Servant King

MARK CHAPTER 11 VERSES 1-33

Some years ago an American pastor, on a visit to London, did the famous sightseeing tour of Buckingham Palace, Clarence House, St. James Palace, Tower of London, etc. That evening he reflected on all he had seen and thought that, as an American, he had no King nor a royal family. It was then it struck him that as a Christian he had a greater King and actually belonged to a greater Royal Family. Motivated by the thought, that evening the preacher sat down and wrote this chorus:

Majesty, worship His Majesty
Unto Jesus be glory, honour and praise.
Majesty, Kingdom authority, flows from His Throne
Unto His own, His anthem raise.
So exalt, lift up on high the name of Jesus.
Magnify, come glorify Christ Jesus the King.
Majesty, worship His Majesty,
Jesus Who died, now glorified, King of all Kings.

Mark wrote this Gospel, not as a journalist nor a biographer giving a catalogue of random events in the life of Christ; Mark wrote as a theologian and as an evangelist and purposely communicated a portrayal of Jesus Christ as the Servant of Jehovah yet as the Sovereign Jehovah. In chapter eleven Mark again displays the humanity and humility of our Lord alongside His deity and authority as the Saviour enters the closing days of His ministry.

Jesus presented as the Messiah to Jerusalem. 11:1-11

The chapter begins with the Saviour coming to Jerusalem. In the last week of His ministry Jesus Christ came to Jerusalem at least three times. The first occasion was here at the beginning of this chapter when he came riding on a donkey and was hailed as a King coming in the name of the Lord in fulfilment of Zechariah's prophecy. (Zech. 9:9) The following day He exercised the authority of a chief priest when He returned to Jerusalem from Bethany and entered the Temple to cast out the money changers and those who commercialised the Temple. (11:12-15) On the third occasion He came to Jerusalem as the weeping Prophet who at the end of three years of ministry wept over the city saying, "O Jerusalem, Jerusalem, thou that killest the prophets, and stonest them which are sent unto thee, how often would I have gathered thy children together, even as a hen gathereth her chickens under her wings, and ye would not." (Mark 11:27, Luke 19:41, Matthew 23:37)

For more than thirty years Jesus Christ lived in the shadow of the cross. During three years of ministry He had done many mighty works. The time drew near to finish the greatest work on earth. Before the end of the week He offered Himself as a substitutionary sacrifice for sin. The week was crowned by His resurrection from the dead. Moreover, this was a week of contrasts.

The week began with Christ riding on a colt; it ended with Christ carrying the cross. The crowd shouted their spontaneous acclamation of Hosannas; soon they showed how superficial was their adoration and shouted their hatred. The disciples flocked to Him; soon they forsook Him. He rode as a Victor, soon they made Him a Victim. He came as a King to the coronation; soon they crowned Him with thorns; They showered him with their praise, later they anointed

Him with vulgar spittle and cruelly nailed Him to the Cross. It was a momentous week.

Through all of this we must keep our eyes fixed on our Lord and His control of every event and circumstance.

The Saviour's might in reserving the colt. In this action, the omniscience of the Saviour shone through. Jesus, who had not yet entered the city, sent two of His disciples, and he not only told them where to go, but also how they would find the colt. He knew the past history of the colt on which no one had ever sat. Furthermore, He foresaw what would be asked of His disciples when they untied the colt and told them how they should reply. The two disciples found all things to be exactly as the Saviour had predicted.

The Saviour's majesty in riding the colt. The Romans were famous for the pomp and ceremony of their victory parades. The coming of the Messiah to Jerusalem was in great contrast. The mount of a horse and tens of thousands of captives were not for him. Instead, the humble colt was prepared; the crowd, mostly Galileans, covered the animal with their garments, and the Saviour descended the Mount of Olives on the donkey. The prophecy of Zechariah was recognised, "Thy King cometh unto thee...riding upon an ass." (Zechariah 9:9) Palms, the symbol of Jewish independence, were strewn in the pathway. The chants of the multitude echoed across the Kidron Valley, "Hosanna; blessed is He that cometh in the Name of the Lord."

The Saviour's meekness in requiring a colt. The famous "Trooping of the Colour" in London is accompanied with the splendour of pomp and ceremony and is spectacular. Until recent years, Her Majesty rode from the Palace to St. James Square on a beautifully groomed black horse. It bore all the marks of royalty and authority. There is no King to compare with Jesus Christ and no authority like His, yet He came on a humble donkey. Entering Jerusalem on a donkey was not just the symbol of humility, it was also a symbol of peace. Soon will come the day when He shall be seen as the Rider of the White Horse with the sword of Judgement in His hand, leading the armies of heaven, and on His vesture shall be written, "King of Kings and Lord of Lords." (Revelation 19:11-16)

The Saviour's mission in returning the colt. The mission of our Lord was not finished when he rode the colt. It was only another step on the way to the cross. When I read about this event, I always remember Pastor William Mullen preaching at the farewell of my colleague Dr. Bill Woods in 1960. The Pastor likened the outgoing missionary to this donkey! "The Lord hath need of him!" The colt was **required** by the Master just as the Lord requires people for His work today. This chosen colt was **reserved** for Christ just as He must hold the reins of our lives today. The colt was **ridden** by Christ and brought Christ to the crowds. No one noticed too much about the colt, their attention was to the One Who sat on it. What a lovely picture of the work of the Gospel preacher communicating Christ to the people. His work is not to draw attention to himself but to the Master Whom he serves. Finally, the colt was **returned** to the man who had first loaned it. If a cup of cold water given in His name shall not lose its reward, what must a colt be worth? What must a life be worth when it is fully given to God? Pastor Mullen's word for Bill Woods was an appropriate message, for his life is one that has been fully reserved to bring the Saviour to multitudes.

Jesus Proclaimed a Curse on the fig tree. 11:12-14

"He found nothing but leaves; for the time of figs was not yet." (Mark 11:13) Some people have objected to this as a negative miracle when Jesus vindicated His wrath on a tree which had no fruit. The Saviour did not need the tree nor the fruit. However, this miracle should not be interpreted as an isolated incident; as we studied in an earlier chapter, Jesus Christ was a great story teller. This was evident from the many parables He told. Moreover, there were times when He did not tell a parable; He acted it. Mark set forth the miracles of our Lord as parables in action. As we have already studied in the miracles of Mark 5, we noted how Mark demonstrated the power of Christ over demons, disease and death. In this last miracle recorded by Mark we find the cursing of the fig tree set alongside the cleansing of the temple. The reason for this is because the cursing of the tree is related to the cleansing of the temple which followed almost immediately.

Normally the fig tree, which often was mentioned as a symbol of Israel, was more productive than any other tree. It gave a large quantity of fruit twice a year, and the fruit normally grew at the same time as the large fig leaf filled out. Where there was no fruit, the leaf grew more lush, but the tree remained barren.

This was a parallel to what the Saviour found in Israel. The Israelites were pretentious in their appearance of worship and ceremony, but these, like fig leaves used by Adam and Eve, only covered the shame of their barren service and naked religion. At Christ's command the fruitless fig tree withered. It was divine judgement. So also the pretentiousness of Israel withered; Jerusalem was destroyed; the temple was burned; the sacrifice ended and the people were scattered. This was divine judgement.

Although this miracle is an historical event and spiritual in its interpretation, it should be looked upon as practical in its application. The Lord still looks for fruit in our lives, and for that purpose we have been chosen. (John 15:16) Alas, our worship and service to Him are too often sterile and fruitless. I recall travelling back to Brazil by boat for our second term of service after a very busy and physically draining furlough. The cargo boat on which we travelled docked for a few days in Bridgetown, Barbados, and we went ashore. Strolling around the Penguin Market at Bridgetown harbour, I suddenly heard a girl begin to sing the hymn, "Nothing but leaves for the Master"; the thought was challenging as we faced the Amazon again. I remember praying, "Lord deliver us from the large leaves of unproductive service that offers no fruit to Thee."

Jesus Purged the Temple. 11:15-21

The Saviour had cleansed the temple at the beginning of His ministry, but again it had been polluted. He entered Jerusalem and found the temple to be a den of commerce and extortion. The temple authorities refused to use the coinage of the Roman Empire which bore the image of Caesar, so they produced their own temple coins for use in offerings, etc. To purchase these coins the money changers charged a costly exchange rate whereby the worshipper lost and the merchant fattened his purse. It was sacrilege and daylight robbery in the guise of religion. The temple was meant to be the house of prayer and the palace of the Living God. With righteous anger, our Saviour overthrew tables and chased the money changers out as He purged His temple. In the next few chapters there is much activity around the temple. Within a week the great veil of the Holy of Holies was torn by the omnipotent Hand of the Lord at the moment Christ cried, "It is finished!" The temple was under the judgement of God, for its service had failed.

Jesus' Promises and Principles for Prayer. 11:22-26

During the last week of our Lord's ministry, He and His disciples commuted between Bethany and Jerusalem. The direct route from Bethany to Jerusalem was over the Mount of Olives, via the little village of Bethphage—"House of Figs." Early on Tuesday morning they came to where the Saviour had cursed the fig tree and found it withered. Peter seemed to express surprise that the tree had indeed died. At that very spot Jesus taught His disciples three crucial lessons.

A lesson on fruitfulness. The fig tree had been a sham of hypocrisy. It was a symbol of sterile religion without substance and empty faith without works. There is nothing so distasteful to the Lord as an empty profession and an unfruitful life. It has been said that the fruit of a Christian is another Christian—a soul won for Christ. There is also the fruit of the Spirit. (Galations 5:22-23) Paul taught the Galations that if we have the right root, we should produce the right fruit. It is interesting that when Jesus spoke of His people being ordained to bear fruit, he followed it by saying, "...that whatsoever you ask the Father in my name, He may give it to you." (John 15:16)

A lesson on faith. The Lord Jesus also taught them a lesson on the assurance of faith, "Have faith in God." When I left work and home to be a student at the WEC Missionary Training College in Glasgow, I was filled with many misgivings and thoughts. I had stepped out to serve God and had no guarantee of from where my support would come or where all this was leading me. However, when I arrived at 10 Prince Albert Road, Hynland, I was challenged by a large text above the front gate of the college, "HAVE FAITH IN GOD." Mr. & Mrs. Rowbotham, the founders of the school, and other dedicated staff and students who lived in that house taught me that to have faith in God was to rest on God's faith and faithfulness. Hudson Taylor also had these words mounted over the headquarters of the China Inland Mission. He translated, "Have faith in God" as "Hold fast the faithfulness of God."

The Saviour continued to speak of faith as being active in prayer. Of this Spurgeon said, "The limit of faith is the will of God; our guides to that limit are the promises of God and the faith which we are enabled to exercise." "What things soever you desire, when you pray, believe." What great latitude we have when we desire the will of God and the glory of God in prayer.

A lesson on forgiveness. Jesus Christ taught us, "When you pray say, our Father." He also taught, "When you pray, believe." Here the Saviour instructed His disciples, "When you stand praying, forgive." We are to forgive because we are forgiven. We are to forgive in the same way we are forgiven. We are to forgive that we might be forgiven. We also are to forgive for our own spiritual growth. Faith and forgiveness are essential to fruitful praying.

Jesus perplexed the Pharisees. 11:27-33

Aristotle, the Greek philosopher, is the man credited with inductive study and education. That is, we educate ourselves by the questions we ask. Another said, "Man raises himself toward God by the questions he asks." Questions are the grappling hooks by which we scale the summits of truth and explore the revelation of God in the Scriptures.

The chief priest, Scribes and elders who came to Christ formed the "Council of Jerusalem," and, as such, were guardians of the Law. If anybody claimed Messianic authority, they had responsibility to investigate the claim. For this reason the Council members challenged the Saviour, "By what authority doest Thou these things?"

The demand the question made. The question had been prompted because of the events of the chapter. Jesus Christ had demonstrated His authority by His entrance into Jerusalem as a King, the cleansing of the Temple as a Priest, and the cursing of the fig tree as a Prophet.

The dilemma the question presented. Jesus Christ answered with a question, "The baptism of John, was it from heaven or of men?" The right answer to this question would have answered their question, but they were caught on the horns of a dilemma. To admit what was true was to concede their unbelief. To answer what was untrue was to condemn themselves. They were caught in their own craftiness and opted to keep silent, but their silence condemned them.

The demonstration His answer gave. In the following chapter Jesus tells a parable in which he demonstrated the authority of the Father, the authority of the servants whom the Father had sent, and finally, the authority of the Son, Jesus Christ. Jesus Christ showed that it was not only a matter of His authority but of their accountability to Him. The finite minds of men may yet ask many questions, but, Jesus Christ is still the only answer to our need.

CHAPTER NINETEEN

Christ Is The Keystone

The Gospel according to Mark pulsates with action in every chapter. The Saviour is constantly moving from place to place on foot with His disciples. He is teaching in the synagogue or by the sea. He is healing in a house or on the road. He is praying on the mountain or casting out demons from helpless victims. He calms the storms at sea or feeds multitudes who are hungry. Suddenly Mark brings us to a point where his account of the miracles of our Lord stops, and the action changes. He moves more slowly as he approaches the climax of our Lord's ministry and sets the scene for the hatred of the religious leaders which would lead to the death of our Saviour.

This hatred was not recent or sudden. From the early days of His ministry, the religious leaders rejected Him and His teaching, and Pharisees and Herodians combined to plot the destruction of Christ. (3:6) Later, after the Saviour cast out money changers from the temple, the chief priests and the scribes consulted with each other how Jesus could be destroyed. (11:18) This antagonism of the religious leaders against the Saviour not only continued, it intensified. Our Saviour met the rejection and hostility of His enemies head on in this chapter—"And they sought to lay hold on Him, but feared

the people: for they knew he had spoken a parable against them."
(12:12) Although surrounded by those who were opposed to Him,
Jesus Christ boldly countered their hostile questions and exposed
their hypocrisy by highlighting their responsibility and ours.

Jesus taught our responsibility to the Gospel. 12:1-12

The parable of the vineyard was familiar to these Jewish leaders.
In Isaiah 5:1-7 Jehovah likened Israel to the vineyard God had chosen and planted in fertile soil. Jehovah asked, "What could have
been done more to my vineyard, that I have not done in it?" Un-
grateful Israel had turned her back on God, and because of this,
judgement followed. The Saviour took up the same theme and set
forth all the elements of the Gospel story.

Besides the many other points that may be majored on in this
parable, it clearly sets forth the moral attributes of God. As the
Owner of the vineyard, there is an overflow of God's love, His good-
ness, faithfulness, patience, forbearance and grace which are shown
to those who repeatedly rejected Him. Likewise emanating from
the same Owner is a demonstration of the Holiness of God expressed
in His righteousness and justice towards those who disobeyed the
Owner and rejected His Son.

The Saviour summed up the parable by asking if they had not
read the final words of the Jewish Hallel which was soon to be sung
at the Passover Feast: "The Stone which the builders rejected is
become the head of the corner." This is a quote from Psalm 118:22-
23 and is alluded to, not only by our Lord, but also by Paul and Peter
in relation to Christ as the Chief Cornerstone. The cornerstone de-
termined the accuracy of the rest of the building.

A Jewish legend tells of when the temple was being built. All
the stones for its construction were symmetrical and prepared at the
quarry face under Jerusalem. As each stone was sent to the temple
site, a careful inventory was kept. One day a stone was delivered to
the site which upon examination was found to be different from all

the others. The stonemasons felt a mistake had been made so they tossed it down into the Kidron Valley. The discarded stone was soon covered with weeds and overgrown with moss as the work proceeded. However, when the time came to lay the chief cornerstone, it could not be found. Enquiries were made at the quarry where the stone should have been prepared. The inventory showed that it had already been sent to the site and that its proportions were different from all the other stones. It still could not be found. Suddenly, someone remembered a stone had been delivered and had been judged to be irregular; therefore, they had thrown it down into the valley. Quickly they retrieved the discarded stone and brought it to its rightful place.

> *Lo, the Stone which once aside,*
> *By the builder's hand was thrown,*
> *See it now the building's pride,*
> *See it now the Corner stone!*
>
> *Lo, we hail Jehovah's deed,*
> *Strange and wondrous in our eyes!*
> *Jesus Christ is Lord decreed,*
> *Bid the voice of gladness rise.*

Jesus taught our responsibility to Government. 12:13-17

Again the Pharisees and the Herodians combined and sent their most accomplished interrogators to try to trap the Saviour with a question. They came up with what they must have thought was a master piece, "Master, we know that Thou art true..." They then got to the burning issue of the day: "Is it lawful to pay tribute to Caesar?" The question was loaded with flattery and designed to ensnare the Saviour in a vexed issue of that time. The Herodians supported the Roman Poll Tax and the Pharisees opposed it as being disloyal to Israel. Cunningly they tried to corner the Saviour. To endorse the tribute was to support the Emperor. To oppose it was to rebel.

The Saviour's reply was magnificent. He asked for a coin. One side bore an image of Caesar, and on the other an inscription of the attributes by which the Emperor claimed to be divine. Jesus asked whose image was on the coin, and they replied, "Caesar's." With devastating simplicity, yet with profound wisdom, Jesus Christ replied, "Render to Caesar the things that are Caesar's, and to God the things that are God's."

The question of Christian responsibility as a good citizen has always been a hot potato for debate. D. L. Moody, the famed American evangelist, was a most practical man. One day he met a man who felt that a Christian had no business getting involved in voting. Moody asked the man, "Are you going to vote in the election?" The man answered with an emphatic, "No! My citizenship is in heaven." "Well then," replied Moody, "I advise you to bring your citizenship down to earth for the next few days." The person who does not vote has more to do with politics than he thinks. In His one line reply our Lord taught the following:

The Responsibility of Government. God is in favour of order, and He founded government which is a proper administration of responsibility. He established the home and appointed government in the home. He bought the Church and established government in the Church. God also founded society and established government and rule in the land. Governments are responsible to God.

Our responsibility to Government. As the Emperor's image is on the coin, so there is a responsibility to Caesar. We are to pay for our government by the taxes we owe. We are to pray for the government to which God has made us responsible.

Our responsibility to God. We are God's coinage, and we bear His image; therefore, we should render to Him what we owe Him. He gave His all for us. Too often Caesar receives what is his due, and God is neglected in our responsibility to Him. Under the same token, we should never give to God and rob Caesar.

Jesus taught Our Responsibility to God. 12:18-40

When the Pharisees and Herodians had spent their cunning skill, Mark reports that the Saducees came with their astute question. As stated earlier, although they were the smallest group in Judaism, they were probably the most influential. They were Zionists who considered themselves to be the brains of society, and they were liberal in their theology. Although they accepted the book of Moses, they discounted the prophets and had little place for the traditions of the Pharisees. As the Pharisees had tried to ensnare Christ, so the Saducees tried to embarrass Him with a well rehearsed question which had confounded theologians for years. They proceeded to tell the story of seven brothers who married the same woman. They followed it with a question, "In the resurrection therefore, when they shall rise, whose wife will she be of them? For they all had her to wife."

Jesus indicted these smart Saducees as being the victims of their own ignorance. They were ignorant of the Scriptures which teach the resurrection, ignorant of the strength of God which accomplished the resurrection and ignorant of the Saviour who secured the resurrection. Not only is the God of Abraham alive, but because He is the living God, Abraham also lives.

Reichel was preparing the choir at the last practice of *Handel's Messiah*. The leading soprano sang the chorus "I know that My Redeemer Liveth" with proper intonation and clarity of voice which left many breathless. However, it was not enough for the Maestro. He asked the soprano, "Do you believe what you are singing? Do you believe that He lives?" The singer replied, "I believe with all my heart that my Redeemer lives." To this the Maestro said, "Sing to make me believe it. Sing to make the world believe it." With added conviction and tears of emotion she sang from her heart what she really believed, "I know that my Redeemer liveth."

Asking questions and discussing deep theological matters was a popular pastime with the people. The Commandments were high on the agenda, and discussing which commandment had priority was a popular point of debate. One scribe who perceived that Jesus answered with great wisdom addressed his question to the Lord Jesus, "Which is the first commandment of all?" In reply our Lord quoted the *Shema* which is the Jewish creed from Deuteronomy 6:4 and linked it with Leviticus 19:18. "Thou shalt love the Lord thy God with all thy heart... thou shalt love thy neighbour... there is none other commandment greater than these."

The Saviour has taught that our love is not for the law but for the Lord, not for the rules and ritual of religion, but for love which is based on relationship to God. Jesus Christ linked our vertical relationship to God with our horizontal relationship to men. We do not live by rules; we live by relationship, and out of the relationship should flow love for the One to whom we are related. He loved us first and loves us longest. Our love is but a response to that heavenly love. Jesus showed that the greatest thing a man can do is to love the Lord with all that he has.

Love is the Sum of all God's Law. If we were able to open and see the heart of the Law, we would find that love would be its centre and substance. When God gave the Law, He gave it for man's good because He loved us. All sin is not so much against the Law, it is against the Lord and against His great love. We best express our love for the Lord by keeping His Word.

Love is the Standard for all living. Where love is lacking there is the empty sound of a hollow life. Calvin said, "A life minus love equals zero." Love will regulate our behaviour, dictate our motives and motivate our service. When we lose our love for Christ, we also lose our love for the Scriptures, for prayer, for souls and for other Christians. Stay in love with Christ, then living for Him will follow.

Love is the Strength of all our labour. Love is the root of fruitful service for Christ. Love for God in our vertical relationship will be evident by our labour for God on the horizontal and human relationships. C. T. Studd said, "If Jesus Christ be God and died for me, then no sacrifice can be too great for me to make for Him." Someone asked, "What does love look like?" They then offered this reply, "Love has hands to help others, feet to hasten to meet a need, eyes to see misery and ears to listen to the sighs and sorrows of other people." Our love for Christ should be the motivation of all our activity and the solution to all our apathy.

Jesus showed our responsibility in giving. 12:41-44

"But she of her want did cast in all that she had, even all her living." The story of the widow and her two mites is one of the most beautiful and touching stories in the New Testament. It stands in utter contrast to the rest of this chapter. Of all the nameless women in female biography, this lady is one we would love to know more about. Yet she is only one of many anonymous people who were prepared to give to Jesus Christ. There was the boy who gave his lunch, the man who gave his boat, the man who gave his colt and the man who gave an upper room. These all stood as challenging contrasts to others.

Dr. Peter Marshall once announced the familiar consecration hymn, *Take my life and let it be*. He requested that the congregation give particular attention to the words:

"Take my silver and my gold,
Not a mite would I withhold."

Explaining the practical implications of the lines, he asked that those who could not sing them with sincerity to refrain from singing. The impact was dramatic. The organ music drifted over the building, but the congregation stood mute. No one would sing, "Not a mite would I withhold."

Mark produced a rare diamond with which to crown this chapter in which there is so much antagonism against the Saviour. In it he showed the Saviour's attitude to our offerings to Him.

Jesus' warning to wealthy professors. Pharisees loved the pre-eminent place. They were proud of what they wore, where they stood, the works they did and the wealth they owned. They were interested in what they got. The widow was interested in what she gave.

Jesus' witness to the woman's offering. Jesus saw the sadness of her widowhood. He knew all about her loss and loneliness. He knew the social difficulties facing a widow in society. He recognised her sacrifice. It would have been a sacrifice to give one mite. Out of love for God, she gave all that she had. Sacrifice is not an attractive word in an affluent age.

Jesus' word to His own disciples. By what Jesus said to His disciples, we note where the Saviour sat—near the treasurery. I am sure Jesus paid more attention to the treasurer than the offerings. He still does. What Jesus saw is equally important. He not only saw the amount given but the attitude and circumstances out which it was given. He still does. Dr. Vernon Magee characteristically remarked of this widow, "The Lord takes the widow's two coppers and exchanges them for the gold of heaven." That was a prudent investment.

CHAPTER TWENTY

Jesus Is Coming Again

MARK CHAPTER 13 VERSES 1-37

P hilip Bliss was one of the greatest hymn writers of the Church. He was author of some of the all time favourite hymns such as, *Man of sorrows what a Name*, *Hold the Fort for I am Coming*, *I am so glad that my Father in Heaven*, and *I will sing of My Redeemer*. These are but a few of his many great hymns.

Born in Pennsylvania in 1838, he developed a great love for music and became an accomplished pianist and organist. In 1869 his path crossed that of the great evangelist of the time, D.L. Moody. Mr. Moody was so impressed with the talents and dedication of Philip bliss that he invited the young musician to work with the Moody evangelistic team. This he did with great effect and blessing. During the next few years Philip Bliss was in demand all over the United States, and besides composing hymns, he was exceedingly used to win many for the Saviour.

In 1876 Mr. & Mrs. Bliss spent Christmas with some friends in Ohio. On the evening of Friday December 29 they took their leave from their friends and boarded the overnight train for Chicago where they were to join Mr. Moody for the New Year services in that city. Mr. & Mrs. Bliss never reached their destination. At midnight, as the twelve car train passed over the high bridge above the Ashtobula River, the poorly constructed bridge collapsed under the weight of the train, and in the darkness of the winter night the carriages plummeted seventy feet into the ravine and the roaring river below. Mr. & Mrs. Bliss had gone to be with Christ.

When news of the catastrophe reached Chicago, Mr. Moody was shattered. On Sunday morning he rose to address those who had gathered for morning worship on the last day of the old year. Tears coursed their way down the evangelist's face and ran into his bushy beard; his heart was heavy and his voice was broken as he gave the news of the tragedy to the congregation. In the stillness of the moment Mr. Moody announced as his text for that morning, "Therefore, be ye also ready: for such an hour as you think not the Son of Man cometh." The text comes from our Lord's Mount of Olive's discourse on His coming again.

Examination of the Scriptures reveals that the Second Coming of the Lord Jesus Christ is one of the greatest themes of the Bible. There is no other topic more persistent in the 260 chapters of the New Testament in which more than three hundred references are made to the Second Coming of the Saviour. Sadly, what should be one of the greatly loved doctrines to unite God's people has been abused and misused to divide us into camps and schools of thought. Some use it to take scalps for their camp as if it were a theological hand grenade on the ecclesiastical battle field. The millennial reign of Christ is one bone of contention. The "post-mil" camp declares that Jesus will only come after the thousand year reign. The "premils" are sure He will come first and then establish His thousand year reign. The "a-mil" group is equally certain that there is no such reign for a thousand years. Others divide as to whether the Saviour's coming is to be "post tribulation" or "pre-tribulation," and some even hold He will come in the midst of the tribulation period. I appreciated hearing Dr. Warren Weirsbie say that he had "long since resigned from the planning committee of the Lord's return and was now a member of the welcoming committee." It is good to bear in mind that we love the Saviour, and it is His appearing for which we look.

This golden theme of the Second Advent of the Saviour was not given to satisfy curiosity and even less to start denominations. It was given by our Lord to instil comfort to the saints. His words in John 14:1-3 was a balm for troubled hearts, and Paul's words to the Thessalonians was to wipe away the tears of those who grieved for their loved ones fallen asleep in Christ. (1Thess. 4:13-18) Even as I write this book, news has come of the death of two New Tribes missionary hostages after many months of captivity in Columbia. Their families, friends and colleagues undoubtedly are devastated by the news, but their grieving is not without hope. These missionaries have won the martyr's crown and will join with all who have died in Christ and those who will be caught up to meet the Lord in the air for the great reunion on the day of His return.

The blessed hope of our Lord's return was also given as an incentive to holy living, teaching us to deny ungodliness and worldly lusts and to live soberly, righteously and godly in this present world. (Titus 2:11-13) John explains that this blessed hope should have a purifying effect on the believer. (1John 3:1-3) However, John also says that the believer who is not pursuing godliness and abiding in love with his brother in Christ will be ashamed of the Saviour at His coming. It is important that when Jesus comes we are not found with dirty hands engaged in dishonest deeds, nor unclean lips profaned by sordid gossip nor our feet standing in places that are not becoming to our calling. Being at variance with a brother in Christ is not only a shame now, it will cause shame when Jesus comes again.

The soon coming of the Saviour is also an impetus to dedicated service to Christ. The Saviour said, "I must work the works of Him that hath sent Me while it is day for the night cometh when no man can work." He warned His disciples against slothfulness and negligence in service so that when the Master returns the servants are not to be found sleeping.

The imminent return of our Lord should sound the alarm to the unconverted. When we were children, we used to play hide-and-seek. One child would close his eyes and count to ten while the others all found a place to hide. When ten was counted, the first child would then warn all those who were hiding, "Here I come, ready or not." That is what Jesus Christ warns the unconverted today, "Surely I come quickly—suddenly!" "Be you also ready."

The Olivet discourse of our Lord is the greatest exposition Jesus gave outside of what we generally call the Sermon on the Mount. It all began when the disciples asked the Lord about the great stones and the magnificence of the temple. According to Matthew, on the way into the city, Jesus had predicted the destruction of the temple. Such a thing seemed unlikely to the disciples who were overwhelmed with the grandeur and seeming permanence of the temple structure. Jesus reassured them that as He had pronounced, so not one stone would be left standing on another in the Temple.

They left the temple and crossed the valley to the Mount of Olives where four of the disciples came privately and asked about the signs and times of the Lord's prediction. Their questions gave rise to the Saviour's predictions and admonitions in this chapter.

Be sure of sudden destruction. 13:1-4

The temple was the glory of Israel and one of the wonders of the world. The destruction of such an edifice seemed inconceivable. Within forty years of the Saviour's prediction, the unbelievable actually happened. The sack of Jerusalem in AD 70 is one of the great dates of history acknowledged by Jew and Gentile. Titus, a Roman General, led his armies against the city. The temple was plundered and burned, and in the ensuing search for melted gold, the soldiers literally pulled one stone down from the top of the other so that temple area was flattened.

The destruction of the temple and Jerusalem was God's judgement on the dead system of Judaism. It was a lesson for the first century and for ours. Peter reminds us that in the last days scoffers will come saying, "Where is the promise of His coming? for since the father's fell asleep all things continue as they were." (2Pet.3:4) Today we look at the things around us, and they may seem so permanent. They will soon pass away and melt with fervent heat. Paul reminds us we are to keep our eyes on the things which are not seen, for the things we see are temporal, but the things we do not see are eternal. The glory of Israel was destroyed.

Beware of spiritual deception. 13:5-6

Great delusion and deception are characteristic of our times. The warning against false Christs was not only sounded by our Lord but also by John, Paul and Peter.   There has never been a shortage of antichrists, for the spirit of the age is antichristian. These only pave the way for the coming of the Antichrist. Presently we contend with the antichrists of liberalism and modernism who speak of a Christ which is foreign to the Scriptures. Their Christ is neither virgin born nor divine in His nature. They say there is no efficacy in His blood and deny the resurrection. This is antichrist. We also encounter the false christs of many cults. Russelites, who wrongly call themselves Jehovah Witnesses, propound a Christ who is less than God. Mormons speak of a Christ who is a figment of Joseph Smith's imagination. Roman Catholicism presents a Christ who is reduced to a wafer in the Mass. Under the cloak of evangelicalism many arise with a false Christ in the gospel of the new prosperity of health and wealth. Jesus Christ said, "Take heed lest any man deceive you."

Behold coming developments. 13:7-28

The Saviour spoke of the developments in coming times. God's calendar and clock are accurate, and He set the agenda of the prophetic programme.

Developments in the world. A study of the Olivet discourse touches on national developments with war between nations, physical developments with earthquakes and tragedies, commercial developments with seeming prosperity as in the days of Noah and moral developments with the breakdown of morality.

Developments in the church. The church will be marked with a departure from the truth—the great apostasy, and the doctrine of demons which will be acceptable to many. (1Tim. 3:1; 2Tim. 4:3) The love of many saints will diminish, and faith will be greatly tried.

Developments in Israel. During the Great Tribulation period the abomination of desolation will occupy the holy place, and Israel will embrace the Antichrist. Great war and destruction will follow before the great revelation of the Saviour. All of this infers the re-establishment of Israel as a nation, the rebuilding of the Temple and the reintroduction of temple worship.

Many of these developments are around us in the bud or in full bloom, and we are to keep our eyes fixed on the coming of the Lord.

Believe in sure deliverance. 13:29-32

Scriptures should be interpreted by the Scriptures. The Bible teaches us that first Christ will come for the saints in the great day of the rapture of the Church when the Lord Himself shall descend from heaven with a shout and with the voice of the archangel and the trump of God. We shall be caught up to be with Christ. This will be a time for rewards at the Judgement Seat of Christ and a time of rejoicing at the Marriage Supper of the Lamb.

The Bible then teaches that Jesus will come with His saints, and every eye shall see Him. Israel shall be delivered and judged; the nations of the earth shall enter into judgement, and Jesus shall establish His great reign.

Be ready for soon departure. 13:33-37

The servant who loves his Lord is not the one who is able to say how far off or how near the coming of the Lord may be. Rather, it is the servant who is ready for the Master's coming. The above explanation is as I see it in my simplistic way. If it does not happened as perceived, that is of no concern to me. What is more important is that we be ready for the coming of the Lord. The word our Saviour repeatedly used in our readiness for His return is the word "watch".

It is the look of a servant who is praying. (13:33)
It is the look of the servant who is working. (13:34-35)
It is the look of the servant who is awake. (13:36-37)

A few years ago a British Midland flight from London to Belfast made a tragic emergency crash landing near to the East Midland Airport. The loss of life was high. In the following court case it was said that the Captain warned the passengers immediately before the crash, "Prepare for an emergency!"

Fellow passengers for eternity, Jesus is coming soon. Prepare for eternity!

CHAPTER TWENTY-ONE

Memorable Hours

MARK CHAPTER 14 VERSES 1-72

V isiting the State Rooms at Windsor Castle was an unforget table experience. We felt the place was rich in history and tradition. Here kings and queens once sat in magnificent splendour and glory. However, when we visited Bethany, we felt that we had come to a place which had even greater significance than Windsor Castle. This small village on the eastern side of the Mount of Olives held us in awe as if we had come to the State Room of the Saviour. It was in Bethany that Jesus often resided at the home of Lazarus and his two sisters, Mary and Martha. It was at Bethany that Lazarus was raised from the dead. It was at Bethany that some of the greatest expressions of love were shown to the Saviour and by the Saviour. Jesus Christ is the Lord of glory; it is symbolic that He came to Bethany, which simply means the "house of the poor." Bethany may have borne the name of the poor house, but it was a rich place indeed.

An Extravagant Love 14:1-9

The chapter has it dark moments of treachery and betrayal, plotting and pain. However, it all stands in perfect contrast to one of the most beautiful incidents in the life of our Lord. When Mary broke her alabaster box and poured the ointment on her Saviour's head, she did it as an expression of sincere and sacrificial love for Jesus Christ. For this the Saviour not only commended her but also commanded that wherever the gospel is preached in all the world, her action should be spoken of as a memorial to her. I venture to say that this commendation of our Lord was not only that her act be recorded for posterity but also that those who would take the Gospel into all the world must be prepared to perpetuate the principle of sacrificial love for Christ. If this be the case then there are some questions worth asking.

What did she do? She did something which was expensive. She broke her alabaster vial of precious ointment and anointed the head of the Saviour. Her action was considered expensive, for it was equal in value to one year's wages. However, it was a full expression of her love for Him. She might well have done it for her brother when he died, or she could have sold it to give to the poor of her town. All these were legitimate causes, but what she did was done exclusively for her Lord. What she did was extravagant, for she irreversibly broke the seal of the box and poured it all on the Saviour's head.

Where did she do it? She did it in the house of Simon the Leper in Bethany. What a table to sit at with Simon healed from leprosy and Lazarus raised from the dead. What conversations must have taken place between the blessed and the Blessed One. Furthermore, Bethany was Mary's home town, and she honoured Christ just where she lived.

When did she do it? Mark gives the date at the beginning of the chapter; he tells us it was near to the Passover and within hours of the passion of the Lord. The enemies plotted and planned with malice against Him how they might destroy Him. His disciples murmured about what Mary did and considered it to be the waste of good money. Did they not think He was worth it, or did Judas have other plans for the money? When the world hated Him most, and disciples were speaking against Mary, it was then that Mary loved Him most. The magnificence of her deed is only matched by the malice of His enemies and the murmuring of His followers

Why did she do it? Was this action by Mary to our Lord not an appreciation of His worth? She realised this was not just a man, this was the God-Man. It may have been extravagant, but she judged Him to be worth it all. Was what she did not an act of her worship and done out of a full heart of gratitude and love? Furthermore, this anointing anticipated His work on the cross. Jesus said it was done against His burying. When Christ was in the agony of the Gethsemene, the fragrance of the ointment still lingered with Him. In the isolation of the judgement hall when all had forsaken Him, the token of Mary's love still gave its aroma. When Christ was cruelly nailed to the cross and His garments were taken as the prize of those who cast lots, the perfume of Mary's ointment still emanated from the Saviour. Mark said the fragrance of the ointment filled the room, and you can almost detect the ancient aroma as you read the story. This was extravagant love.

An Evil Betrayal 14:10-11.

There are many names which spell out infamy and evil. Stalin, Hitler and Mussolini are only a few of the notorious names of recent history. However, there is no name more despicable or more treacherous than that of Judas Iscariot. Here in Brazil, children are named after all the other disciples and Bible characters, but no one ever calls their child after Judas. Sadly and ironically, he had a name which was glorious—Judas means praise; yet he turned out to be a misfit of history and a tragedy to humanity.

Like a sombre valley of gloom between two mountains of glory, Judas' betrayal stood in great contrast between the display of love for Christ in a home in Bethany and the demonstration of the Saviour's love for us at the passover table in Jerusalem. Mark purposely penned another dark hue in the masterpiece portrait he gave us of the closing events of the Saviour's life.

The Prophecies that predicted Judas. The Psalmist foretold that a near friend would betray the Lord (Psm 41:9) as well as the loss of his office. (Psm 109:8) Zechariah predicted the price paid would be that paid for a crippled slave. (11:12-13) If Judas had been familiar with the Bible, he could have seen himself in the prophecies.

The privileges that were poured on Judas. The honours he enjoyed and the privileges he received threw his treachery into greater disgrace. He was a follower of Christ, called to be an apostle, a preacher, the treasurer of the twelve, had his feet washed by the Lord and was made an honoured guest at the table with the Twelve.

The plot which was planned by Judas. He planned and executed the plot to betray the Lord. Sadly, it had never cost him anything to follow the Lord, and he was a covetous and greedy man. He did the Devil's work.

The price that was paid by Judas. He followed the Light of the world yet walked in darkness. He kissed the Gate of Heaven and went to Hell. He sold the Saviour and his soul and paid his own way to hell. Wasted privileges and lost opportunities may never return.

An Enduring Memorial 14:12-25

At sunrise on December 7, 1941 350 Japanese planes flew out of the morning sky over Pearl Harbour and rained death and destruction on the famous naval base. Besides the eighteen battle ships and 200 aircraft which were destroyed, over 3500 American service men were killed or wounded. President F.D. Roosevelt called it "a day of infamy." With that the United States entered World War II. Throughout the war when American service men needed motivation, the cry went up, "Remember Pearl Harbour!"

Our Saviour instituted a memorial feast whereby we are to remember Him. The Lord's Table, instituted at the Passover feast in a borrowed upper room, is the touch stone of our faith. The symbols Christ used were symbols of Jewish deliverance out of Egypt in the Passover Feast.

The Bread. In the midst of the meal Jesus Christ took the unleavened bread and said, "Take eat: this is my body." Jesus was not indicating this was His literal body. These were simple symbols then, and they are still symbols now. Bread was always a symbol of life. The Saviour gave the bread indicating He was giving His life for them. His life was a sinless life, and His death was a sacrificial death. As we partake of the bread we identify our faith in the sufficiency of that sacrifice which was made once and for all for us.

The Cup. In the Passover meal there are four cups. The Cup of Sanctification was to remind the Jew they were a chosen and sanctified people; the Cup of Blessing was a cup of gratitude for the blessing God had given to the family over the preceding year; the Cup of Redemption symbolised the price which was paid by the blood of the Pascal Lamb for their deliverance out of Egypt; the Cup of Hope was to look forward to the coming of Messiah. It was precisely at the Cup of Redemption that Jesus instituted the Lord's Supper.

This Cup of Redemption became the symbol of the New Covenant and our Redemption in the blood of Christ. The rich redness of the wine reminds us of His atoning and precious blood. The pouring of the wine reminds us He poured out His life unto death. We drink the wine and remember His blood was spilled for us. The memorial feast continues until Jesus comes again. "I will drink no more of the fruit of the vine until that day that I drink it new in the Kingdom of God." (14:25) Soon we shall drink of the Cup of Hope at the Marriage Supper of the Lamb.

An Evening Song. 14:26

"And when they had sung a hymn they went out into the Mount of Olives." (14:26) Handel's *Hallelujah Chorus* is almost universally known. It's famous climax of repeated "Hallelujahs" has brought countless thousands to their feet in great admiration and applause. "Hallelujah" is a combination of two words; *Hallel* which means "to boast" or "to praise," and *Jah* which is Jehovah. Therefore, Hallelujah simply means "Praise you Jehovah!" or "make your boast in Jehovah."

The *Hallel* is the name given for the Psalms sung during the Passover Feast and are made up of the Psalms 112-118. We therefore know the hymn sung by our Saviour and His disciples before they went out into the clear night on the way to Gethsemene. It was Psalm 118. The Saviour often referred to this Psalm, and the final verses are filled with poignancy and meaning when considered they were the final words the Saviour would sing before going to the cross.

"This is the Lord's doing." (Psm. 118:23) Having finished the supper in which the symbols of death and sacrifice were shown, and before He stepped out into the night of anguish under the eastern sky, our Lord sang with confidence that this was all God's doing.

"This is the day which the Lord hath made." (Psm. 118:24) What a day lay before the Saviour. The hours ahead of Him were hours of anguish and sorrow, hours of mocking and beating. Within twelve hours He would be whipped, spat upon, crowned with thorns and nailed to a cross. Yet, He joined the others to sing, "This is the day the Lord has made; we will rejoice and be glad in it."

This is the Lord's devotion. "Bind the sacrifice with cords, even unto the horns of the altar." (Psm. 118:27) Ahead of Him was the cross. He saw it as the altar where He would die as our Substitutionary Sacrifice to bring us to God. Although nails pierced His hands and feet, He was bound with the cords of love and devotion on the cross. He sang all this within the shadow of Calvary.

An Extreme Agony. 14:32-52

"And they came to a place which was named Gethsemane." (14:32) As we near to the climax of our meditation in Mark's Gospel, we come to the almost untouchable and incomprehensible mystery of the passion and death of our Lord Jesus Christ. His birth at Bethlehem was a mystery to heavenly angels as they beheld the Son of God incarnate. His years of obscurity in the carpenter's shop in Nazareth were a mystery, for He was God incognito—hidden from human view. His life was an enigma to his contemporaries. However, at His passion and death, it was as if holy angels hushed their voices and heaven waited in silence to witness the great finale as Jesus Christ perfected the work of our redemption. Who can ever measure or describe the depth of agony, the height of pain, the length of endurance or the breadth of love shown by our blessed Lord in Gethsemane, at Gabbatha and on Golgotha.

Gethsemane—It was an appropriate place. The name Gethsemane means "oil press." The place was appropriate, for here olives were crushed to pulp so that the rich oil could be extracted. Jesus Christ was crushed between the severe mental anguish as a man facing the hellish malice of Satan as wells as the Father laying on Him the sin of the world.

Gethsemane—There was agony in this place. Disciples accompanied Him to this final place of prayer, but the Saviour was alone when He cried in agony to the Father. The place of prayer became the place of pain. Matthew reminds us that the pain was "exceedingly sorrowful." Mark says He "was sore amazed and very heavy unto death." In this garden our Lord resisted unto blood and in agony of soul the monstrous assault of the Devil. Luke writes of the Lord "being in agony" and the "great drops of blood" which emphasise the depth of suffering of our Lord. Our sorrowful, sore, suffering Saviour was covered in the crimson blood of His own sweat. Did ever angels or men see such a sight?

The Effective Prayers. 14:39

"And again He went away and prayed." (14:39) One of the great reformers in the history of the church was John Knox. It was said that so piercing and cutting were Knox's words that the infamous Bloody Mary, Queen of Scots, feared the Scottish reformer and banished him from the pulpit at St. Giles Cathedral in Edinburgh. However, John Knox was not only a powerful preacher, he was equally fervent on his knees in prayer. Mary once remarked, "I fear more the prayers of John Knox than all the combined armies of Scotland."

No one ever prayed like Jesus did. He was both eloquent and · authoritative in his preaching, but what must the prayers of our Saviour been like? Never was there a voice heard that was more exalted, more holy, more fervent, more fruitful or more intense than that of Jesus Christ on that night in the Garden of Gethsemane.

His prayers were offered with great suffering. The writer to the Hebrews gives an insight to the prayers of our Lord in Gethsemene. "Who in the days of His flesh, when He had offered up prayers and supplications with strong crying and tears unto Him that was able to save Him from death, and was heard in that He feared; though He was a Son, yet learned He obedience by the things which He suffered." (Heb.5:7-8) In the garden Jesus Christ faced Satan who tried to put the Saviour to death some other way than the cross.

His prayers were short, simple and yet so strong. Again quoting from Hebrews, the prayers of our Lord were "prayers and supplications with strong crying and tears." Prayer must not be measured in the immensity of words but in the intensity of heart. Many times the disciples had heard Jesus pray, but never had there been prayer like this. Strong praying resisted Satan. His fear was not the fear of death but the fear He might die before the cross. It is not just that Jesus died that mattered, but that He died the death of the cross.

His prayers were with complete surrender. "Not my will but Thine be done." The Saviour in His prayer spoke of "the cup" and "the hour." These are terms He had used repeatedly in anticipation of Calvary where He would be made sin for us. Jesus Christ held nothing back. He fully surrendered and fully submitted Himself to the will of the Father. Our sins were the burden He bore at this pinnacle of prayer.

His prayers were always successful. The prayers of our Lord were always in accord with the Father's will. Bible gardens merit our attention and meditation. The history of the human race all began in a garden, and history will finish in the Eden above. The

Saviour prevailed in His great work in the Garden of Gethsemene. In the first garden, Adam was in rebellion against God. In this second garden the Saviour was in submission to God. In the Garden of Eden, Adam lost all because of his disobedience. In Gethsemene Jesus gained all for us by His obedience. The tragedy that was sustained in Eden was reversed in Gethsemene.

An Example of Failure 14:66-72

Peter's pen did not write this Gospel, but his finger prints are found in almost every chapter. He was Mark's informant and the source of much of the foundation data which was also used by Matthew and Luke. Peter was open and honest about his own flaws and faults while he exalted his Lord; this teaches us a great deal about his character. He never forgot the hot tears when he wept at having failed his Saviour in the hour of rejection.

Often failure in our lives is not the act of a moment. It is the erosion of our devotion and the drift of self indulgence, and then we suddenly find we are far from our Lord. Mark traced the drift in Peter's downfall through a series of steps in this chapter. Peter boasted too early that he would never forsake his Lord. (14:29) Peter slept too easily when it came to the watch and pray in the garden. (14:37) Peter acted too hastily when the soldiers came to arrest the Saviour. (14:47) Peter, with the other disciples, forsook his Lord too readily at the hour of the Saviour's passion. (14:50) Peter denied His Lord so insensibly with oaths and curses. (14:66-71) Is it any wonder he wept bitterly when he realised how far he had drifted? (14:72)

It is told of Alexander the Great that in his sweep toward power and world domination he came to Jerusalem. The inhabitants waited in terror aware of Alexander's great army and the trail of blood left in their wake. Josephus records that when he came face to face with the Jews, Juddua, the High Priest, robed in white garments, went out with other priests to meet the conquering army and its leader. Juddua took from a sheath a scroll and read chapters seven and eight of

Daniel's prophecy. These chapters foretold the conquests of the Greeks over the Persians and the greatness of their leader. When Alexander saw himself in the Scriptures, he spared Jerusalem and treated the Jews with dignity.

Like Alexander, we also should endeavour to see ourselves in the Scriptures. Too often we highlight Peter's rashness and failure. He was a great man. He made his mistakes, and some of them were bad enough to make him feel all washed up as a servant of God. Yet, he was honest enough to admit them and humble enough to weep his way back to the Saviour. Do you see yourself in Peter?

CHAPTER TWENTY-TWO

The Mistrial Of Jesus Christ

MARK CHAPTER 14 VERSE 53 - CHAPTER 15 VERSE 15

D uring the last world war there was forged between Great Britain and the United States what Churchill dubbed as The Great Alliance. However, during the same war there was another alliance which might well have been known as the Unusual Alliance. Churchill and Roosevelt sat down in conference with Stalin in the holiday spa at Yalta on the Black Sea and made what became known as the Yalta Agreement. What was unusual about it was that nations which had been arch enemies earlier in the war became sudden friends and were united in a common cause to destroy Hitler.

There was also another notorious Unusual Alliance forged in the final days of our Saviour's life. Those who had been arch enemies of Christ formed an uncommon and unholy alliance against Him. Individually the participants of the alliance were easily identified.

The religious conspiracy of the Jewish Council. Motivated by fear and envy, the elders of Israel plotted against the Saviour. He did not conform to their traditions, and His authority in word and deed threatened their power. He had exposed their hypocrisy, condemned their empty formalism and cleansed the temple. This was their hour as they punched him, spat on Him and falsely accused Him.

The intellectual contempt of the learned Scribes. Jewish life was shaped and regulated by the Mosaic Law as interpreted by the Talmud. Scribes knew the Law and the Talmud, yet Jesus Christ was railroaded to rough justice with their consent.

The political conduct of Pilate. Before the Jewish court, Christ was charged with blasphemy and was without guilt. Before the civil court the charge was treason, and Pilate could find no fault in Him. There were strange allies in Jerusalem when Jesus was tried. Sadly His own had forsaken Him and fled.

Each party contributed and accommodated the other and so accomplished their common aim—the death of the Saviour. One such partnership already existed between the Pharisees and the Herodians since the early days of the Saviour's ministry. Herod supported Rome and all things Greek; Judaism opposed all foreign influence. Again unholy hands joined in a conspiracy to annihilate our Lord. First, there is the coupling of Herod and Pilate who had been avowed enemies of each other, but here they were made friends. Add to these Caiaphas joining with Caesar and declaring publicly, "We have no King but Caesar!" Caiaphas and Caesar and Israel and Rome were strange bedfellows indeed.

THE JEWISH TRIAL

As we look at the events which surrounded the trial of our Lord, we are struck with the whole atmosphere: the fear of the Jews, the treason of Judas, the panic of the disciples, the treachery of the High Priest and in the midst of it all, the serenity of the Lord Jesus.

Seven hundred years earlier Isaiah had written of Him, "He was despised and rejected of men, a Man of sorrows and acquainted with grief. He was led as a lamb to the slaughter and as a sheep before her shearers is dumb so He opened not His mouth."

The injustice and hatred against Jesus. Our blessed Lord was railroaded to judgement which was unfair, disorderly and illegal. No person was ever more innocent. No trial was ever so false. No crime was ever so wrong. In all our Lord faced six trials. There were three religious trials: one before Annas, one before Caiaphas, and one before the Sanhedrin. There were also three civil trials: one before Pilate, one before Herod and then back to Pilate again. Before the Jewish court the charge was blasphemy, but before the Roman court the charge was treason.

Why were there so many trials? Under Roman rule the Jews were not permitted to administer capital punishment. For this reason the Jewish authorities turned Jesus over to the Romans, and our Lord was crucified under Roman law and not stoned as in Jewish Law.

Jewish life and tradition had been moulded and regulated by the Mosaic Law as interpreted in the Talmud. However, even by their own standards, Jesus received grievous injustice. Here are a few of the laws as outlined by Dr. John MacArthur which were conveniently overlooked and ignored by the Jewish authorities.

1. Arrest for a capital crime must be made in broad daylight and not at night.

2. Arrest for a capital crime could not be made on the information of a follower because his follower could be counted as an accomplice to the crime.

3. No Jewish trial was to be held at night, from dusk to dawn, and no trial for a capital crime was to be conducted during a feast.

4. Members of the Sanhedrin after hearing testimony regarding the one accused of a capital crime were not permitted to give an immediate verdict. Justice demanded they first return home for two days and two nights. Only then should they hear again the testimony against the accused before giving their verdict.

5. Sanhedrin members must only vote one at a time beginning with the youngest.

6. All witnesses against the defendant had to be questioned separately and all must agree in detail before the evidence is admitted.

7. No one person could act as judge. A verdict could only be reached by a court of at least three people, twenty three people or seventy three people.

The Sanhedrin kept breaking their own procedural laws in what became a gross miscarriage of justice in a kangaroo court. Annas was the father-in-law of the current high priest whose name was Caiaphas. He had served as high priest for seventeen years. He was undoubtedly the wealthiest and most influential man in Israel. He owned and operated the money changing system which was corrupt to the core, and ever since Jesus upset his business in the temple court yard, Annas had a personal vendetta against Jesus. Even in the rending of his garments the priest disobeyed the Law.

The insult and humiliation of Jesus. The crowd was guilty of making the wrong choices, and they had to live with those choices. The blood of Christ was on their hands. While it was true that they put Jesus on trial and delivered Him to be crucified, the truth is, it was really the Pharisees who were on trial. Their choices sealed their fate.

The injury and the hurt of Jesus. All through the unjust and humiliating trials of our Lord, His qualities shone through. There was always evidence of His innocence. When false witnesses were brought before Him at the High Priest's palace, they only indicted themselves, for one witness contradicted the other. Even Pilate was forced to confess that he could find no fault in Him.

Added to His innocence was the Saviour's silence. Our Lord never cried out in defence of Himself even though He had every right to. Rather, by every step to the cross He left us an example of how to bear up under suffering unjustly imposed on us. Peter said of Him, "When He was reviled, reviled not again; when he suffered, He threatened not; but committed Himself to Him that judgeth righteously." (1 Peter 2:23) His silence and serenity were the products of the confidence He had in the Father's plan.

When we understand the trials of our Lord, we see how small our own tests are in comparison. Peter, as we noted had forsaken the Lord at this hour. Later he explained that we were all called to be like Jesus who gave a good confession before Pontius Pilate and left us an example to follow in His steps.

CHAPTER TWENTY-THREE

The Cross Of Christ

MARK CHAPTER 15 VERSE 6-37

Key Hole Kate was the name of a character in children's comics some years ago. As you might imagine she was noted for being nosy and gleaned most of her information by peeping through the key holes of the neighbours houses. Today we use her technique in reverse. Many homes, for security, are equipped with a spy hole which permits the resident to view who is at the door. A keyhole or spyhole may have a small aperture, but much can be seen through it. There is a parallel to this in the Bible. Some Bible statements may be brief, but they open up a panorama of truth. When Mark wrote, "And they bring Him unto the place Golgotha," he gave us such a keyhole to look through. (15:22) To the casual reader, the verse may seem simplistic, yet the more we look into it, we find a mine of truth begins to open to us.

Such a depth of meaning and height of truth are found in these words. Earth had never witnessed a scene like it before. Never had so many ever poured such hate and contempt on One Who was so innocent. They hounded Him like baying dogs hunting for their chase. In their frenzied hate they surrounded Him; they mocked Him and demanded He be made the victim of the most barbaric death. Their hideous and grinning faces spelled out their scorn. Their mocking eyes stared at Him as they hurled their cruel words of scornful taunts. So detestable was the spectacle that heaven would not endure the scene. At high noon the sun suddenly hid its face, and for three long hours the wicked crowd groped in the darkness of midnight at midday. The earth convulsed beneath their feet; rocks were rent; graves were opened and an invisible hand rent the veil of the temple. It was a day of infamy and a day of shame, yet for all believers, Golgotha is the cross-roads where time and eternity meet. Here heaven met earth, and here God still meets the repentant sinner.

Calvary was God's masterpiece. The scenes must have been horrific. But, the cross was the altar. Jesus Christ was the Lamb. The blood was the price of redemption. We are the benefactors. Mark writes of Calvary not to appeal for pity but as a call to faith in Jesus Christ.

The path that led to the cross

The path that leads to the cross is sometimes called the Via Dolorosa. However, as we have suggested on other occasions, that pathway to the cross started long before Jesus Christ left Pilate's judgement hall.

The Commencement of the Pathway. On the Isle of Patmos John learned "He was the Lamb slain from before the foundation of the world." (Rev.13:8) Calvary was no accident of history. It was no invention of the Devil nor the after-thought of God. Rather, in the plan of the God's eternal counsel, Christ was sent forth for this very hour. Golgatha was by divine appointment for "Him, being delivered by the determinate counsel and foreknowledge of God, ye have taken and by wicked hands have crucified and slain."

The Course of the Pathway. When Moses and Elijah met with Christ on the Mount of Transfiguration the subject of which they spoke was of Christ's death. Christ's death is the great theme of the ages. It was first taught to our parents before they left Eden when their shame was covered by the sacrifice of animals. Abel learned about the death of the sacrificial lamb in his time. Noah and Abraham, the Passover and the Tabernacle—yes, the Cross threw its shadow over every page of history.

The Cruelty of the Pathway. Mark wrote, "And so Pilate, willing to content the people, released Barabbas unto them, and delivered Jesus, when he had scourged Him, to be crucified." (15:15) Never before had there been such a display of human guilt. Never before had there been such a manifestation of Divine grace.

Consider the scourging. Roman scourging was a terrible torture reserved for the worst criminals. The Saviour's hands were tied behind His back, and He was tied to a block which forced His back upwards. The whip was a long leather tong studded with sharp pieces of bone. Thirty nine lashes were then applied to the back, and every lash shredded the flesh and reduced the body to raw bleeding pulp. The Saviour gave His back to the smiters.

Think of the stripping. Having survived the scourging, Roman soldiers thought nothing of mocking a Jew. They laughed Him to scorn because He claimed to be King. They stripped Him of His clothing, robed Him in purple and then crowned Him with platted thorns. He was worthy of diadems, but He took the thorns of our sin.

Reflect on the smiting. They took rods and beat Him, undoubtedly puncturing the brow where sharp thorns pierced through. They plucked the hair from His face. He knew the name of every soldier, and soon He would bear their sin to the cross.

We may blush at the spitting. Having crowned Him and robed Him, there was no oil to anoint Him as King in the mocking game. Instead of oil, mocking soldiers displayed their own depravity as they emptied their throats and spat upon Him. "Bearing shame and scoffing rude, In my place condemned He stood." All His suffering was not designed to arouse our pity but to assure us of the extent of His love for us.

John Bunyan wrote in his immortal **Pilgrim's Progress** how Christian, on his way to the Celestial City, focused his gaze on the cross. As he did he felt the burden he carried on his back begin to loosen and fall from him. It rolled down the hill and disappeared into an empty tomb. The burden symbolised all his guilt and his fears of coming judgement. It was then that Christian cried out "O blessed Cross! Yea, rather, blessed be the Man who there was put to shame for me." The cross and the Saviour who died for us is the glory of the Christian.

The Climax of the Pathway. Jesus said, "The hour is come that the Son of Man should be glorified" (John 12:23) He spoke of being crucified as equal to being glorified. This was the way our Lord had to come, and He endured the cross, despised the shame and is now set down at the right hand of the throne of God.

The people who came to the cross

A range of people stood around the cross that day. There were mourners and mockers, soldiers and civilians, religious zealots and rebels, women weeping and many mocking..

Simon of Cyrene carried the cross for Christ. He was compelled to come to the cross. (15:21)

The soldiers brought the nails, the board, the paint. It was their duty to be at the cross. (15:20)

Two thieves brought their sins to the cross. From the cross one died in faith and went to Paradise. From the same execution the other died in sin and went to hell. (15:27-28)

The scorners brought the vinegar and the sponge to add to the suffering of the victim. (15:23)

John the Apostle brought Mary the mother of the Saviour to the cross.

The priests and scribes brought their insults to the cross. When all rational argument was exhausted and found wanting, insult and scorn were the only means left. (15:31-32)

The people watched him as a spectacle on the cross and passed by pouring out their scorn. (15:29-30) It was reported that during the French Revolution one of the things which astounded many is that the ladies were able to bring their knitting to watch the executions by guillotine.

The Centurion brought the spear which punctured Christ's side. At the cross he discovered that Christ was God. (15:39)

The sympathetic women brought wine and myrrh. They came to stay at the cross. (15:40-47)

A preacher prepared to preach on the cross; he dreamed the night before he was to preach. He saw the nails driven into Jesus' hand, the crown of thorns on His head and the sword thrust into His side. He could bear it no more, and he ran to grab one of the soldiers. When he swung the soldier around, he found it was his own face he was looking into. He was there to nail Jesus to the Cross. In a sense, we all were there.

The Person who died on the cross

It was a mystery that He could die. He was the Son of God, the Eternal Word who had created all things and given life to every man.

It was a mystery that He would die. Paul said it well, "Scarcely for a righteous man will one die: yet peradventure for a good man some would even dare to die. But God commendeth His love toward us, in that while we were yet sinner, Christ died for us." (Romans 5:7-8)

It was mystery that He died as He did. Crucifixion was an ingenious and horrible death cruelly devised by the Romans and

155

one of the crudest forms of death ever contrived. Even in the Roman world it was reserved for only the worst criminals of the time. In His death He joined in the company of common thieves and took the place of a certain Barabbas who was worthy of the cross. Even while on the cross, he prayed for those who nailed Him to the cross and instructed John to care for Mary.

The price that was paid on the cross

"Without the shedding of blood there is no remission of sin." There was no other way to put away sin other than by the sacrifice of Himself. He took our sins on His body on the tree and was made the propitiation for our sins whereby divine justice was satisfied making it possible for the sinner to be justified.

Jesus Christ gave all for us and did everything necessary for our salvation. He is therefore worthy, and we in return give all to Him. Frances Ridley Havergal was a great lady. Among the many things she did was write some beautiful hymns for the church. One day she penned her sentiments and thoughts about Christ in verse. When she was through, she was not happy with what she had written; she threw it in the waste paper basket. Someone in the house picked it up. They not only kept it but had it published. Here are the words.

Thy life was given for me
Thy blood O Lord was shed.
That I might ransomed be
And quickened from the dead.
Thy life, Thy life was given for me:
What have I given for Thee.

CHAPTER TWENTY-FOUR

Dealing With The Dead

MARK CHAPTER 15 VERSES 38-47

During my pastorate at Templemore Hall I had an ongoing friendship with the local undertakers. One morning at a funeral the undertaker asked me how things were going at the Hall, and I told him they were fine and numbers were encouraging. I asked him how things were with him, and he replied, "They are going well, and the numbers were good!" I did not know if he was speaking about his church or his job! Another local undertaker invited me to a function he had organised. When I got there I was appalled. He was inviting me to use my position to try and sell "prepaid funerals" to the members of the church. (I was absolutely convinced he knew little of the hazards of pastoral work!) All arrangements were to be made before the person dies and this would enable the person to arrange his own funeral—even as far as picking the coffin and paying the bill. I need hardly tell you I declined the offer.

The Lord Jesus Christ was not only in control of His own death, He made His own funeral arrangements. John was the only disciple who stood at the foot of the cross. He recorded in his Gospel that to speed up the death of the victim, soldiers came and broke the legs of one thief and then of the other, but when they came to Christ they found that He was already dead. To ensure that he had not just passed out, a soldier thrust a spear into Jesus' side, and from the wound there came out blood and water. This was one sure sign of death. Here was the separation of dark red corpuscles and the thin light serum from the pericardium. This indicates that the heart must have been punctured by the spear.

Christ was dead. What a day! What a moment! The events which surrounded the death of our Lord were quite remarkable: the darkness, the rending of the rocks, the raising of the dead, the cries in the darkness. Yet, of all the events that surrounded the death of our Lord, the most devastating to Judaism was probably the rending of the veil in the temple.

The damaged curtain in the Temple. 15:38

The rending of the veil. Marks gives details of the Saviour's death by "the hour." He informs us that the Saviour was crucified at the third hour—9:00 a.m. Darkness came on the scene at the sixth hour—noon. It was at the ninth hour—3:00 p.m., that Christ cried out with a loud voice, "It is finished." In that precise moment, the ninth hour, the veil of the temple was rent in twain from top to bottom. It was precisely at this hour that the priests were ministering in the temple. You can you imagine as they stood before the altar of incense, suddenly and dramatically, they heard an almighty roar as the curtain, the thickness of a hands breadth, sixty feet high and thirty feet wide, was ripped in two from top to bottom.

Not only was the hour at which it happened significant, but the hidden Hand that tore the curtain was also significant. The timing reminds us that God was watching every detail of the drama on Calvary, and when the work was completed, God testified from heaven by rending the veil in two. Furthermore Mark used the terms "from the top to the bottom." This hidden hand could not have been that of a man. Only God could have torn it from the top to the bottom. That it was ripped right to the bottom indicates how severe and complete was the rending. It was not a partial tear but a total severing of the curtain.

The temple priests were divided into twenty-four courses, each one ministering for one week at a time. For twenty-three weeks they had no temple duties until the cycle of twenty-four weeks came round again. However, during Passover week all twenty-four courses were in full attendance at the temple. This meant that when the veil was torn and the mercy seat became visible, many priests looked on it for the first time. Is it any wonder that when the apostles preached in the power of the Holy Spirit that many priests believed the message of the Gospel? (Acts 6:7) They had seen the effect of the finished work of Christ.

The requirement of the veil. There was only one way to God and that way was through this veil. It was the final separation between God and man. The temple contained a whole series of barriers and restrictions. There was a wall which limited Gentiles from approaching even as far as the Jews. Yet another wall restricted the approach of Jewish women. Another division at the entrance to the Holy Place kept Jewish men out, and only priests were admitted. The last barrier was this veil which separated the Holy Place from the Holy of Holies where only the High Priest could enter once each year on the Day of Atonement.

The removal of the veil. When the veil was torn, there were no more barriers to God. No more veil or separation existed. Therefore, no priest was needed; there was no more need for an altar of sacrifice; no more lambs needed to be slain; no more blood needed to be spilt. God put out the flame of judgement which had burned on the altar. A New Way was now opened by which men could come to God in Jesus Christ. Every day we have the blessed privilege of approaching God, and "Where e'r we seek Him He is found and every place is hallowed ground." He is the Priest, the Altar, the Sacrifice and all we need.

The discerning Centurion at the Cross. 15:39

Here is a man of whom we know little. We do not know his name, how old he was or if he was married or single. We do know that he was a soldier in Caesar's army, but we do not know if he was a seasoned campaigner or a novice, a volunteer or a conscript. The only distinguishing thing we know about him is that he is the man who crucified Jesus. At least two men trusted Christ at the cross. One was a Jew who cursed Him and the other was a gentile who crucified Him.

That day the Centurion crucified Christ. He had never met such a person as Jesus Christ. Never had he witnessed such derision against a person and yet such devotion to the same person. When the sun darkened and the earth shook, he stood amazed at things which he had never witnessed before. Often he had heard curses, blasphemies and all sorts of threats from screaming victims, but never had he ever heard a person pray on the cross.

That day the Centurion was converted to Christ. Within hours of commanding soldiers to drive in the nails to crucify the Saviour and watching his men gamble for Christ's garment, something happened in the life of this Centurion. Although he knew little about theology, he made one of the clearest statements about the identity of Jesus Christ, for he openly confessed that the Christ of the cross was the Son of God.

Mark had good reason to include the account of this Centurion. He was addressing his writing principally to Romans who were commanded to reverence the deity of Caesar. Many perhaps had asked questions about the deity of Jesus Christ. Mark presented a Roman Centurion who gave the answer. Here was a seasoned soldier in the Imperial army who had seen Jesus Christ close up, and even though he was a Gentile, yet he was convinced who Jesus Christ was and he was converted to Christ at the cross.

The distressed company by the Cross. 15:40-41

Around the cross were some friends of Jesus. The majority of them were women from Galilee. They came to weep because of the Saviour, but they also came to be witnesses to the fact that He really died. Had there been breath yet in His nostrils, they would have made every effort to resuscitate Him.

The very women who lingered at the cross and witnessed His death also helped in his burial and were witnesses of His resurrection. The funeral of Jesus was simple. His body was wrapped in linen cloths; spices were placed in this cloth, and He was buried the same day as He died. A very small number attended the funeral service, probably only six, Joseph, Nicodemus, Mary Magdalene, Mary His mother, Mary the wife of Cleophas and John. To attend to the remains of a person who had been crucified as a person guilty of sedition was to jeopardise one's life. That is one of the reasons why the disciples had distanced themselves from the Saviour once he became a prisoner and was charged with an offence. The small company had their own service in a Garden. No songs were sung, and no one gave an oration. Those who loved Him went home broken hearted.

The distinguished citizen who took Jesus from the cross. 15:43

Joseph of Aramithea was a rich man and undoubtedly a religious man. He was a companion of Nicodemus, and both of them were members of the Jewish Parliament, the Sanheidran. He came from the little town of Aramithea, just six miles from Jerusalem. We are not told when or how he came to Christ, but the Bible does inform us that he was a disciple. He, with Nicodemus, appeared to have been secret believers. We do not read any words he ever spoke, but his actions speak eloquently of his love and devotion to Jesus Christ. Dr. Campbell Morgan points out that from the hour of His burial, none but loving eyes looked upon Him, and only tender and dedicated hands ever touched Him,

He was constrained enough to persuade Pilate to deliver the body of our Lord to Him.

He was committed enough to pay for the expensive spices with which they embalmed Christ.

He was courageous enough to dismiss public opinion, and when friend and followers forsook the Saviour, he laid Jesus' body in his tomb.

Was he was confident enough to lend the tomb to Jesus Christ? According to the Saviour's promise, He would occupy the tomb for only three days.

The story is told of an ophthalmic surgeon who opened a practice in London. After some time he realised that no patients seemed to be interested in his services. He became very discouraged until one day he met a blind man, and upon examining him said, "I believe I can restore your sight." The doctor performed an operation on the blind man, and it was a complete success. The blind man was also a poor man, and he knew he could never repay the doctor. "I haven't a penny in the world and can never repay you for what you have done," he said to the surgeon. The doctor replied immediately to the patient, "Oh yes you can. Go and tell others you were once blind, but I gave you sight!" He did, and after that hundreds of people sought to benefit from the skills of the surgeon.

CHAPTER TWENTY-FIVE

Jesus Christ Is Alive - For Us And Forever

MARK CHAPTER 16 VERSES 1-20

C hurch historians credit the great Protestant Reformation to three men: Martin Luther, John Calvin and John Knox. Luther carried the torch which lit the fire, Calvin the pen which gave it theology and Knox the sword which made it last. However, all three men were subject to times of depression and swinging moods. Although Luther brought revival to Germany and had flamed enthusiasm into thousands who were freed from the bondage of Romanism, yet he had times of deep melancholy and despondency when he tormented himself about inward guilt and doubt. It is reported of Luther that on one occasion when he was in such depths of despair that Catherine, his wife, feared for his personal safety and health. She decided to do something dramatic to change his mood.

Dressed totally in black mourning apparel, she arrived in his presence like a grieving widow. Luther quizzically looked at his wife and asked who had died. Catherine announced, "I assumed from your behaviour that God must have died, for if He were alive there would not be reason for such gloom!"

The news of the living, risen Saviour is the climax of Mark's Gospel. It also is the centre of the church's creed, comfort in her sorrow and the inspiration of her conflict. Only a living Saviour is able to save us. Only a living Saviour can comfort troubled and grieving hearts. Only a living Saviour can give strength and power to His people. Only a living Saviour can give us hope and assurance for the future.

The first news of the resurrection of Jesus Christ from the dead was given that first Easter morning by an angel to three devoted women. Mark draws attention to the role of women in the final days of the Saviour's life and then in the first hours of His resurrection. On the verge of His passion Mary had anointed Him with spikenard as an expression of love. (14:1-9) The women from Galilee stood by the cross when the disciples of our Lord had all forsaken Him. (15:40-41) Mary Magdalene and Mary, the mother of Joseph, went to the tomb with Joseph of Arimithea where Jesus was wrapped in linen clothes. (15:47) Here, at first light on the resurrection morning, three devout women came to the tomb to anoint the body of our Lord. In doing so they were exposing themselves to reprimand by the Roman and Jewish authorities for associating with the body of One who had been crucified as a criminal. Their devotion to Jesus Christ is still a challenge to all Christian women in their consecrated service to Jesus Christ.

A series of surprises and shocks awaited these ladies that morning. First, out of devotion they came to the tomb but were preoccupied about how they would gain entrance to the burial chamber because of the heavy stone which blocked the entrance. They need not have worried, for the stone was already rolled away. Second, on entering the tomb they were surprised and frightened to meet with an angel who had the appearance of a young man dressed in a white robe. Matthew said his appearance was "like lightening" while describing his clothing as "dazzling." His appearance and clothing were startling, but the message he gave was even more surprising and sensational for the women. The women might well have been surprised to find an angel attending to the Lord after the crucifixion. During the hours of mistrial, suffering, shame and crucifixion no angel came to His aid. Did they feel the angel had come too late?

They were also shocked to find the body of the Lord missing. "Do not be afraid; ye seek Jesus of Nazareth, who was crucified. He has risen. He is not here; see the place where he lay. Go and tell His disciples and Peter that he is going before you into Galilee; there you will see Him as he told you." The angel's words were designed to calm their fears.

The message of the angel sets the tone of the whole chapter. First, the angel spoke to comfort them in their distress and sorrow. Second, the angel's assurance was designed to instill confidence where there had been doubt, for he announced to them that Jesus Christ was risen from the grave even as He had promised. Third, the angel commissioned them to go and tell the disciples and Peter that He was alive and was going before them to Galilee. This message summarises what in effect happened in the rest of the chapter.

Comfort for Mary Magdalene. 16:1-9

If ever a woman loved the Lord Jesus it was Mary Magdalene. The Lord had transformed her life. At one time she had been possessed by seven demons which led her into all manner of sin and wickedness. Jesus Christ had set her gloriously free. In the New Testament there are five occasions in which Mary Magdalene was in contact with the Saviour. By far the sweetest scene of all these is that when Mary met Jesus Christ on the resurrection morning.

The despondency she felt. As far as Mary was concerned, Jesus Christ was dead. In Him she had placed all her faith, all her hope and all her love. Now He was dead. She could not see beyond the tomb. Paul said to the Corinthians, "If Christ be not risen, we are of all men most miserable." That was the misery which Mary felt. The darkness within her was greater than the darkness around her in the pre-dawn of that day. She was in the depths of despair. Life is only worth living when there is something and someone to live for, and the Person for whom she lived was gone. With the loss of Jesus Christ she had lost the purpose of living. Things could never take the place of the Saviour.

The difficulty she faced. "Who shall roll us away the stone?" It is necessary to remember that New Testament tombs did not have doors. Burial chambers were caves, and stones of various sizes were rolled over the arched entrance. It was not uncommon for these stones to weigh up to a ton. Such a tomb belonged to Joseph of Arimathia. Furthermore, the Pharisees had appealed to Pilate to secure the grave. Besides securing the grave, Matthew reminds us that they set a seal on it. This seal was a cord which passed over the widest part of the stone and was secured to the rock on either side by a clay seal. If anyone should disturb or break the seal, they would incur the wrath of the Roman authorities.

It is unfitting to think that the soldiers who placed the stone rolled it away. Most certainly the Pharisees would not remove the stone, nor did the disciples who were living in fear. It would be impossible for women to roll away the stone. Who then moved the stone? Matthew explains, "And behold there was a great earthquake, for the angel of the Lord descended from heaven and came and rolled back the stone from the door and sat on it." (Mat.28:2)

Frank Morrison was highly educated and a well known English lawyer. He was not a church goer, for he was extremely sceptical of anything relating to Christianity. So great was his scepticism that he decided to write a book to disprove that Jesus Christ was miraculously raised from the dead. He did not know that although he set out to write a book with the intention of destroying the Christian faith, he would in fact write a different kind of book. That book, "Who Moved the Stone," turned out to be a defence of the resurrection and the Christian faith, and resulted in the conversion of Frank Morrison to Christianity.

Heaven has the answer to all earth's problems. Mary with her despondent friends saw a great difficulty in the stone which blocked their entrance to the tomb. This great difficulty was removed when God rolled the stone away and admitted the ladies to the tomb.

The discovery she made. "They saw the stone was rolled away." Not only did she discover the stone was removed but also the Saviour was missing. She did not realise the significance at the time, but it would have been disastrous for her and for all of us if she had found the body of our Lord.

That stone was rolled away not to let the Saviour out nor to let an angel in. It was removed that they might discover that Jesus Christ had risen even as He had promised. We see a progression when we compare Scripture with Scripture about the first resurrection day. In John 20:1 we are told Mary Magdalene came when it was yet dark. Had there been a sleepless night? We are further informed from Matthew 28:1 that the two Marys came as it began to dawn. Mark here reminds us that they came at sunrise. The progress is from the darkness to the dawn and right through to daybreak. Mary had arrived in the darkness of her despondency but had stayed long enough to find the full blaze of glory on that resurrection day.

Some modern versions of the Scriptures omit Mark 16:9-20 excusing "these verses are not found in the best manuscripts." If that were the case, it is inconceivable that Mark would finish His action packed Gospel with the tears of Mark 16:8. It would leave the book unfinished in the gloom of despondency. The Holy Spirit is not only the Author of the Book He also preserves the Book. The Gospel is not complete when it ends in fear and tears. Instead of the tears of frustration, the final verses of Mark offer the triumph of the resurrection. Furthermore, everything we find in verses 9-16 is in total harmony with the other Gospel writers as well as with the contents of Mark's Gospel. No new doctrine is introduced, and no major doctrine is changed or diminished in these verses.

The glory of that Easter morning changes hopelessness to blessed hope, and Mary's gloom and despair to the glory of the Living Christ. An artist once painted a rather gloomy picture. It showed a wild mountain scene. Perched high on the slopes of the mountain was a log cabin. It was dusk, the sky was streaked with black and grey. It was a most dismal looking scene. When one of the artist's friends commented on the bleakness of the painting, the artist was not offended. He just took his brush and with yellow paint put the light on in the windows of the cabin. Instantly the scene was changed from one of gloom to one of glory.

Confidence for the Disciples. 6:10-14

The attitude of the disciples was characterised by stubborn unbelief. Not only had they forsaken Him and fled prior to His death, but they had no faith in the repeated promise He had given them that after His death on the third day He would rise again. Twice Mark reminds us that they refused to believe either the message of the women that Jesus had risen or the testimony of two who had met with the Lord in the way. (6:11-13)

Mark permeates the account of the resurrection of Jesus Christ by three strands of infallible proof.

The absence of the body of the Lord. "He is not here!" The empty tomb in itself was not evidence that he had risen. The only thing the tomb could say was that He was not there. Some would afterwards invent that Jesus had swooned in the weakness of His suffering, and when he was revived he rolled away the stone. Such a thought was absurd, for the stone was sealed from outside. Others would allege that his body was stolen by the disciples. Would they preach with such fervour afterwards and die as martyrs for a cause they knew to be a lie? If the enemies of the Lord had been able to produce a body, they would have done so to destroy the forthright testimony of the apostles about the resurrected Christ.

Although noone witnessed the moment when God raised Jesus Christ from the dead, yet the silence of the empty tomb declared that Jesus Christ had conquered death and had been raised from the dead.

The assurance of the angel's message. An angel is but a messenger. His message was brief, startling and yet very specific, "Ye seek Jesus of Nazareth, who was crucified; He has risen, He is not here." This message from the angel was crucial. Without it they would have known that He was not there, but they would not have known he was risen.

The appearances of the Saviour. Taken over the whole record of the resurrection there are eleven appearances of our Lord, yet Mark here limits the appearances to three. First, He apeared to Mary in the garden. Second, He appeared to the couple on the way to Emmaus. Third, He appeared to Peter and the disciples. Mary had lost the One she loved. The couple had lost their hope. The disciples had lost their faith.

The disciples had been totally devastated with the events of that week. They had started out so confidently with the Saviour's entrance into Jerusalem and all the promise of the coming Kingdom. It all seemed to go so wrong with the arrest, trial, suffering and death of the Saviour. Mark said that they were weeping because of their dashed hopes. When Jesus Christ appeared, He reprimanded their unbelief and proved to them that He was alive even as he had promised to be several times before He died.

Today we do not need to prove the resurrection, yet we do need to be reminded that the resurrection of the Saviour proves many things to us.

The resurrection substantiates that Jesus Christ is the Son of God. The empty tomb could not be accounted for apart from it being a mighty declaration that Jesus Christ was the Son of God. (Romans 1:4) Beyond the empty tomb, there was also the testimony of all who met Him in His post resurrected state. They saw and testified that He was the Son of God.

The resurrection authenticates every claim Jesus Christ ever made. The resurrection is the touchstone of Christianity. If there were no resurrection, then the Saviour who promised and predicted that He would rise again from the dead fooled us, and we are liars. But Christ is risen indeed. (1 Cor. 15:12-20) His word was true, and we preach the Gospel of a glorious resurrection.

The resurrection demonstrates that all power belongs to the Saviour. The Saviour defeated Satan in the desert when He was tempted and in Gethsemane when He resisted Satan unto blood and with earnest pleading. Finally, in death Jesus Christ destroyed Him who had the power of death. All power in all the universe belongs to the Saviour. (Mat.28:18)

The resurrection also corroborates there is a resurrection for us. (1Corinthians 15:20-23)

Commission for the Church. 16:15-20

After the Saviour reprimanded the unbelief of the disciples and affirmed His resurrection, He did not forsake them. Although they failed miserably, yet He employed the very same men for the greatest mission on earth—taking the gospel to every creature. It should be remembered that this was only a small band of frightened disciples. They had no political influence, no religious clout, no financial base and no academic prestige. On the contrary, they were up against the political might of Rome, the bigotry of the Jews and the scepticism of the Greeks. To these men Jesus Christ said, "Go ye into all the world and preach the Gospel to every creature." This command of our Lord has frequently been called the Great Commission. There are many reasons why it should be called the great Commission.

It is great because it fulfils the greatest Mission. Jesus said, "Go." A few verses later we read, "and they went forth." April 14, 1912 was a dark night for East Belfast. It was the night the *Titanic* sank on her maiden voyage. Survivors were appalled to see that some were content to be saved, and they did not care who was lost. Nearby to the *Titanic* was another vessel with the radio turned off. The *Californian* said if they had received the message they could not have gone because "In the darkness of the night we feared icebergs and were lying motionless. For this reason we banked our fires and had no steam up." Alas, today that is the story of the church: no fire, no power; today in the church we have many who are keen to preach but not so many who are keen to go. We must not divorce "the preach" from "the go!"

It is great because it is fuelled by the greatest motive. Paul said, "The love of Christ constraineth me." C. T. Studd said it best, "If Jesus Christ be God and died for me, then no sacrifice can be too great for me to make for Him." Besides the love of Christ, other motives compel us; a lost world is waiting for the Gospel, and our Lord is returning soon. Mollie Harvey was a valued colleague. She pioneered with Mr. & Mrs. William McComb the work of Acre Gospel Mission. Her book "Treasures of Worth," tells of some of her missionary experiences in the Amazon. The title of her book summed up the motive of her long life. She lived for heavens treasures. Let us also show our love to Christ by obeying this His great command.

It is great because it furthers the greatest message. The Gospel of Jesus Christ is the good news of great salvation based on the greatest sacrifice ever made—the atoning blood of Christ, by the greatest Person Who ever lived—Jesus Christ, and it gives the greatest hope to men in their greatest need.

Alas, there has been no great urgency by the church of Jesus Christ to obey this Great Commission. When President John Kennedy was killed by assassins' bullets in November 1963, the tragic news of his death was relayed round the world within an hour of the incident happening. Sadly, the good news of the Saviour's death and salvation in His name has not yet been told in all the world after almost two thousand years since He went to Calvary. Bishop Taylor Smith visited Westminster Abbey. As he walked down one of the aisles, he came to the tomb of David Livingstone. He read these words on the tomb of the missionary explorer, "Other sheep I have." As he stood there the Bishop asked the Lord a question which is worth pondering. "Who shall bring in those sheep if we do not offer our feet to go?"

In the first chapter Mark spoke of "the beginning of the Gospel of Jesus Christ" with the coming of the Saviour to the Jordan River. The Gospel ends with His church going into all the world and the Lord working with them.

As I finish this book, I am in the small town of Tarauaca, almost three thousand miles from the mouth of the great Amazon River. This land is a far distance from the Roman readers to whom Mark originally wrote. However, the Gospel of which he wrote is still fresh, relevant and is the power of God unto salvation for all who trust in Jesus Christ. Furthermore, the Lord is still working with those, who like Mark, have dedicated their lives in bringing the Gospel of Jesus Christ to even this distant part of the world.